EXCUSES, EXCUSES

EXCUSES, EXCUSES

The Politics of Interracial Coupling in European Culture

Larry D. Crawford
(*Mwalimu A. Bomani Baruti*)

Ankoben House
Atlanta, Georgia

Cover Illustration by Charles Nelson

ISBN: 0-9678943-6-0

Ankoben Press
P.O. Box 10786
Atlanta, Georgia 30310

Printed in the USA by
Morris Publishing
3212 East Highway 30
Kearney, NE 68847
800-650-7888

For

Pearl Ward, Bessie Gordon, Mollie McKissic, Lizzie
Patterson, Hattie Mae Chambers and Laura Conners

Frank Crawford, Ellis Chambers, Sr., Simon Chambers
and Paul Crawford

and

the lineages of strong Afrikan women who selflessly
gave their love and lives to their people, and the
lineages of strong Afrikan men who understood and
chose the daughters of these Afrikan women for their
complements/soulmates.

Acknowledgments

I would not be without Odumankoma, the Abosom, the Nsamanfo Nananom and my immediate ancestors. Our elders who have earned the title of Elder by leading us in the Afrikan Way have my utmost respect and appreciation.

My complement/soulmate, editor, friend, inspiration, personal intellectual trainer, spiritual interpreter, loving, patient, forgiving, selfless wife Layla is the strength of this work. Imani Nube, our daughter, is the life of our home who constantly demands that the passion of an Afrikan warrior scholar be reflected in my every thought, word and deed.

This work would never have manifest without the "knowing" of Mama Hill whose spirit still empowers my quest for Afrikan knowledge.

These thoughts are deeply indebted to those Afrikan warrior scholars who formed my family of friends, colleagues and students over these years. Your questions and concerns deserve the clarification that for me could only have truly come beyond the pale of negro institutions.

Table of Contents

Chapter 1. INTRODUCTION

In that every utterance carries with it a political agenda, this book is unquestionably and without apology a political statement. No effort will be wasted claiming some unrealistic and impractical objectivity or political correctness, except to the degree that an objective subjectivity and political correctness can claim an Afrikan center. I claim that Afrikan center. Compromising the will and intent of the ancestors is to be without merit or honor.

This statement was developed primarily for those brothers and sisters who are contemplating a genocidal treason because they have been deceived about the nature of European cultural politics. They have been miseducated about the pervasiveness and persuasiveness of white supremacy in their daily thoughts and deeds. It is for those who sit on the edge of sanity unaware that their free will to choose to be themselves, to be Afrikan, is systematically kept from them by an involuntary socialization in an alien and alienating culture. This is to let them know they do not have to choose Western culture. We do not have to settle for the European interpretation of reality.

Those of us who recognize that the battle is won or lost in the mind are already aware of this problem. We realize that if western motives and symbols can only be dissected, decoded and revealed for what they are, we would already be far in the battle to dislodge this disruptive and divisive wedge from our community. More than anybody else, however, these thoughts are designed to reassure and encourage those who feel that this battle is already or nearly lost. They are committed to the struggle against self-defeating notions that fighting is futile because so few in our community dare openly confront this behavior for what it is and too many of us readily follow whoever and whatever will feed us, no matter the consequences for our children, no matter its contribution to the destruction of Afrikan family and community.

John Henrik Clarke always believed that one of the greatest problems facing our community's drive toward a self-determining empowerment was allowing others to equally participate, and exercise power, in our family debates. He is not alone. His insight remains incisive and relevant. In these chapters, we will focus on the excuses most used by those who invite intruders into too many of our bedrooms. We can not and should not "get over it" as many of these perpetrators advocate.[1] This is family business. And the Afrikan family is far from dead or assimilated into this European madness. Stable families never harbor their enemies, no matter how human they appear.

With that in mind, this book is not designed to address the morality or ethics or desirability of interracial pairing. That is irrelevant outside a deep understanding of the historical conditions under which it occurs. Our only purpose here is to simplify the confusion inherent in the explanations too many participants give for their involvements. As indicated by the book's length, the politics of morality that shape Western consensus is not a topic we need to spend a lot of time on. Debate for the sake of debate is distracting and wastes precious time. We simply need to expose the weaknesses in these excuses from an Afrikan center and move on with nationbuilding. There are casualties in every war. But we must do everything in our power to keep their numbers from growing.

Another qualifier is that we will focus almost exclusively on the Afrikan male. Our analysis will expose the excuses most often given by the lost souls of this population who attempt to rationalize their mentacidal and genocidal infatuation with females in white skin for what they are. Our ancestor Bobby E. Wright defined as mentacidal the thinking of those Afrikans whose mentality reflects the white supremacist interests of the European.[2] Mentacidal individuals not only believe their enemy is their tried and true friend but adopt and implement their friend's genocidal tactics against their own people. Not only do they think as the European, they become the European. When not actively engaged in destroying the will and spirit of our people, the mentacidist wastes an inordinate amount of time trying to appeal to his/her enemy's nonexistent, unless self-serving, morality as a means of appearing to save Afrikans from him/her. As the suffix "cide" connotes, these individuals are brain dead to any Afrikan way. Askia M. Touré does justice to the definition of genocide as the systematic removal of one people from the planet by another in the "Introduction: Holocaust and Human Sensibilities" to his *From The PYRAMIDS To The PROJECTS*.[3] Haki Madhubuti agrees.

> Indeed our time *is* marked on the white calendar. An issue not often discussed is that the United States has never ratified the *Genocide Convention* voted on by the United Nations in 1948. This Genocide Convention has been ratified by the great majority of the world's nations but the "land of the free and home of the brave" refused to pen its name to it. If it did it would probably be no more than a symbolic gesture. However, the important element here is that the United States does not find it necessary to hide its real nature and intentions.[4]

In the Afrikan community this genocide is primarily focused on the male. And, this is for good reason. Unjust or not, the male is seen as the only real potential political, economic and military threat in a culture where men only fear men. Therefore, what some might otherwise call a limited focus on males in this book is intentional. It is very important in a society where males still retain a privileged role as the primary breadwinner and defender of the home.

At the same time, the condition of a majority of our female soulmates make this focus necessary. Being Afrikan and female and being pulled below the poverty line have virtually become synonymous.[5] As recreational drug use and abuse increased with the so-called war on drugs, the feminization of poverty is a process that "workfare" will do little but escalate.

Historically, the highest to lowest rank order of incomes in this society remains European male, Afrikan

male, European female, Afrikan female. Within these
race-gender groupings, the greatest gap exits between
males and females, with the smallest between Afrikan
and European women. Even though this is changing
with the growing obsolescence and marginalization of
the Afrikan male in national and global labor markets
(where the distance between Afrikan males and both
Afrikan and European women is shrinking while the
distance between the European male and both groups of
women remains relatively constant), that order still
holds. The only exception to that rule has produced a
shifting of the race-gender order. In this special case
the order is changing, again from the highest to the
lowest, from European males to Afrikan females to
European females to Afrikan males. Those workers
having the necessary combination of education, skills
and experience who are forming the cutting edge of this
new occupational order have completed their
undergraduate college education and worked at least a
few years since then.

> ...the median income for college graduates 25
> and younger ["with one to five years on the
> job"] was about $18,000 for white men, $17,000
> for black women, $16,800 for white women and
> 16,400 for black men.[6]

Remember that this currently only applies to this
specific category of individuals. However, the impact of
this trend should not be lost if we remain cognizant of
the increasingly service oriented, degree requiring nature
of western labor markets. In other words, because

Afrikan females are increasingly getting more bachelor degrees than Afrikan males, they will increasingly get more of the lucrative jobs than their men. Interestingly, this contradiction in a sexist labor market applies for no educational-occupational category among Europeans. It is important to understand here, especially in light of the income of Afrikan males as "the primary breadwinner" and economic power, that the Afrikan woman has to date brought in a larger proportion of the family pie than any other group of women. It also bears noting that any campaign to resocialize Afrikan women to seek out mates among lesser paid Afrikan men will be long and tedious, regardless of historical precedence. Homogamy, the universal fact that people tend to marry at the same, or very similar, class level, rules. The process of convincing Afrikan men to accept Afrikan women as the primary breadwinners in a nonexploitative capacity may likely take even longer.

For these many reasons, the chapters in this book most specifically address Afrikan male-European female liaisons. Their coupling absolutely and relatively dominates the interracial dating and marriage scenes.

Yet, we know that our enemies and those among us they have confused will always find drawbacks to any truth we prove. So in knowing that there is no end to the excuses people will come up with to rationalize their choices, we have to recognize that no analysis can be complete for some of us. Nonetheless, the basic logic behind the criticisms presented in the following chapters can be successfully applied to any of the less popular or developing excuses also.

As a sociologist and cultural historian it is important for me to point out the impact of the group on the cultural socialization of an individual's decisions. Isolating particular individual choices, as if individuals developed their desires, skills and personalities in a vacuum and not families, groups and society, and whether intentional or not, ignores the social conditioning individuals go through that fits them into the culture. All people are socialized. It is a lifelong process. There is no such thing as a feral child in the European classic sense of being raised in the wild by gorillas, dogs or coyotes. Tarzan is a European fiction. Humans socialize humans.

People become who they are through interacting with others, conforming their behavior to a cultural standard. They are educated through the rewards and punishments applied by significant others. All societies and groups socialize their members to conform to its cultural personality. This method for tracking preferences and dislikes equally applies to individuals who are preoccupied with involving themselves in interracial relationships. It is even more necessary to grasp the significance of this social process when we systematically analyze the thoughts and behaviors of such persons who are already dying to jump in any and every bed with their oppressor for any and every other reason they can possibly manufacture.

The last point that needs to be made in this introduction is that some readers already have been and will remain confused about who in the world I am talking about because of the language used. Many will have a problem with my use of European to describe the general culture in this society. They will have difficulty grasping the idea that this society's culture is European culture. It is.

EXCUSES, EXCUSES

It is mind boggling how so many of us are of the impression that the u.s. is not New Europe. We assume that somewhere in the middle of the Atlantic Ocean the culture changed to the degree that this nation became unique and relatively distinct from the European cultural family. This belief, along with the loyalty that allowed them to be validated in the first place, has even led mainstream Black scholars to argue that "we" in the u.s. are either absolutely no longer Afrikan or that what Afrikanisms remaining are negligible. Many others, Afrikan scholars to the bone, tend to agree with one of our most consistently dedicated warriors.[7]

Kwame Ture, that most dedicated Afrikan warrior scholar who just returned to his honored place among our ancestors, thoroughly agrees.

America, in fact, is nothing but Europe. The white people in America are not Americans but in fact Europeans. When we call them Americans we allow them to escape; we define them incorrectly. We should call them Europeans and understand that they never belonged in America, that they took that continent from somebody else. When you call them Americans you forget that they were Europeans, because you give them in fact the theory of native origin, that they came out of America. Where did Americans come from? They came from America – that is, somebody you call American. But if you say they are Europeans (which is what they are), then the question arises as to where they came from –

8

Introduction

Europe.[8]

For those still in question I suggest beginning a serious, objective study with John Henrik Clarke's *Notes for the African World Revolution*,[9] Marimba Ani's *Yurugu*,[10] Amos N. Wilson's *The Falsification of Afrikan Consciousness*,[11] Kwame Agyei and Akua Nson Akoto's *The Sankofa Movement*,[12] Kobi Kazembe Kalongi Kambon's *The African Personality in America*,[13] Jacob H. Carruthers' *Intellectual Warfare*[14] and Erriel D. Roberson's *The Maafa & Beyond*.[15]

As a result of this confusion we have become so locked up in patriotism and loyalty to European nation-states that we forget that Afrikans are one people. I agree with Ayi Kwei Armah. "I prefer not to forget several thousand years of our common history because of a few centuries of separation."[16] That twenty-six plus thousand years of Ta-Merrian, Saisian, Puntian, Alkebu-lanian, Nubian, Kushite, Ethiopian, Kemetic, Egyptian, Malian, Songhaian and Ghanaian community makes it imperative that we use the terms Afrikan and European to distinguish us from them. "A people's name is a powerful force."[17]

For those who find it necessary to visualize in terms of melanin, or lack thereof, Black is synonymous with Afrikan and white with European. For the more patriotic, African-American and American could be matched with Afrikan and European, respectively.

The words chosen to identify the two groups in this work are no more limiting than the terms plant and animal. Realistically, as historical fact and future vision, Afrikan and European speak to race as culture. However small the proportion interracial couples are of all marriages, the demographic patterns they exhibit in

9

this society reflect the global trend. But, always needing to be first, the heart of Babylon only leads the way.

In the tradition of great race men and women like Marcus Garvey, Sojourner Truth, John Henrik Clarke, Martin R. Delany, Charshee McIntyre and Ida B. Wells who did not forsake their Afrikanity because the designation was unpopular among Europeans, or their colored cultural clones trying to use colorlessness and multiculturalism as survival propaganda, Afrikan and European are naturally used to identify the two cultural-racial groups under discussion.

And, in terms of multiculturalism, we must consistently see beyond the cultural politics. For while the European concept of multiculturalism suggests it seeks to add more meaningful color to the cultural palate, in reality it does not. The historical view through the eyes of participant-victims of European aggression is omitted keeping the palate colorful but harmless to European cultural hegemony.

> But most importantly for many African-centered scholars, the American culture is seen as a culture of tyranny which admits only certain elements from non-Anglo-Saxon culture and eliminates practically all true human elements from the non-European populations, especially the African inhabitants. Much of what is included from these powerless populations is either fabricated or mutilated by the dominant culture.[18]

Erriel Roberson clears some of the political landscape by distinguishing between a eurocentric multiculturalism and a global multicentrism, a difference between

10

Introduction

"infusion" and "transformation," respectively.

...multiculturalism, or multicultural, by definition simply means that multiple cultures are *represented* and makes no specification as to whose *perspectives* these multiple cultures are viewed from. Consequently a textbook curriculum could technically be multicultural, because it deals to some degree with other cultures, and still be Eurocentric in its interpretation of information....Multicentric by definition means the representation of multiple cultures from multiple "centers" or perspectives....Thus, implicit in the word multicentric is the representation of multiple worldviews or perspectives, a specification that is absent in the definition of multicultural and must be specifically articulated as a component of the concept.[19]

So let us be clear. There is a major difference between being a racist and being a race-(wo)man. The former imposes their will on others. The latter imposes their will on self.

11

Chapter 2. I JUST FELL IN LOVE

"I just fell in love," of course, is the most popular answer for why Afrikan males pursue European females. It is an excuse which evokes the most heartfelt sympathy and human understanding. And, rightfully so. Humans are emotional as well as social and spiritual creatures. "I just fell in love" is the oldest and most innocent reason for mating in European society. Emotionally charged mating drives, being culturally identified, defined and directed, place the thoughts of individuals beyond blame. The rationale "I just fell in love and didn't see color," however, is nothing less than a recycled political adaptation of this oversimplified reasoning. It is a social trend constrained and directed by European cultural politics.

For this reason and because too many among us think and act as Europeans, it is also the most difficult excuse to critique. For people do believe they just fall in love in this culture. A few even do become captured by the mind, spirit and physical presence of their soulmate. But they do not fall. Too many of our own scholars, who should know better, who have been trained in the pervasiveness and persuasiveness of culture in the individual's thinking, consciously or blindly push oversimplified European explanations for love. And they do this while ignoring the cultural method behind the madness affecting the choices people make. Two, whose contribution to this confusion should not be forgotten, submit their opinions. Earl O. Hutchinson, in his *The Assassination of the Black Male Image*, does a good job in promoting the idea that these choices are not culturally grounded.

> Most of the guys that marry white women don't do it because they think these women are Green Goddesses, forbidden fruit or possess mythical status. Nor do they marry them because they are lustful or filled with self-hate. They marry them for the same reason black men marry black women. They share common interests, and they love them.[1]

Although both book titles would imply that a statement is being made that will strengthen Afrikan manhood, not dilute it, Robert Staples does likewise in his *Black Masculinity*.

> Many black men and white women mate for no more complex reasons than meeting, liking each other as individuals and choosing to transcend the societal barriers to their relationship.[2]

It is not that simple or simple minded. The outcome resulting from this so-called expert testimony has specific results. And the results impact society regardless of the conscious or blind motivation behind these politicized assertions.

14

Another, J.A. Rogers, went around the world to prove this.[3] Despite his immeasurable contribution to reconstructing Afrikan history he, like many "objective" scholars, had a subjective, vested interest in proving that people "just fell in love." But, as my father, whose expertise like so many of our elders is taken from the everyday, living reality of human experience, once said, "You can fall in love with a dog." And, since you can fall in love with anybody or anything, choice is involved. Love may be where you find it but culture determines where you look. Nothing social, that is having to do with the interaction between two or more people, exists or is interpretable outside of a cultural context. Lest we forget, European culture is notorious for manipulating people's choices in such a way that it looks as if by free will they are independently determined to destroy themselves.

The fact is that Black men are addicted to white women and the results have been a kind of cultural diabetes. The union, temporary or permanent, of the Black man and white woman, is a source of severe sickness of both parties involved. Because their union means that either they have fallen naively in love and are willing to brave whatever storms as a testimony of their love for one another, or they genuinely believe that bullshit pitch about America being a democracy with every man having the right for the pursuit of happiness, or they feel that by marrying into the opposite race they can better help things, or they are completely ignorant of the history of this republic. [4]

15

What we conceive of as love in this cultural context is usually not love at all. At every level, it tends to cloak infatuation and/or socially sanctioned relationships within which one can exercise power over another person.[5] In fact, if we study history closely, we will find that *romantic* love is of recent origin. It was mass produced during Europe's industrial revolution about two hundred years ago in the effort of capitalists to further exploit the incomes of the unsophisticated young laborers who were running from the isolated, abusive, rural patriarchy of their fathers to the urban factories.

From this some will wrongly assume that no true love, like no true civilization, existed before the European. The Afrikan tradition of love between a woman and a man is neither exclusive nor individualistic. And it is a phenomenon still inadequately explained by the bulk of the hundreds of volumes discussing it.[6]

Tradition does not mean archaic, outdated or useless. It means tried, tested and true. "Tradition implies fundamental. Tradition encapsulates history, which is the kernel of culture."[7] Culture evolves out of tradition. Culture is a people's accumulated appreciation of those things and ideas that have ensured their survival and solvency. Tradition speaks to those beliefs and practices that have stood the test of time of a people.

For Afrikans, tradition was created out of a spiritual and cultural science that found and fitted universal law to the organization of society. For European society, tradition is theft. It is the art of fabricating originality so as to seem to have worth. In order for the West to project itself as the culmination and pinnacle of human culture its concept of chaotic progress must replace ordered tradition. Old must be interpreted as bad and new as good. This inverted and divisive dichotomy is reflected throughout western science and popular culture.

Our elders teach us that true love comes only after you've been with someone the many years it takes to *know* that that person would willingly die for you. With an understanding of the mentacidal desires behind the excuses under discussion, an Afrikan centered analysis of this love between a man and a woman would be most appropriate. It is a communal, nation building perspective, that places the spirit of the people first. Essentially,

> ...each partner is willing to give up certain aspects of himself or herself for the advancement of the people. Thus, the relationship is taken out of the individual context and placed into the collective context becoming a part of the generative will of the people....A visionary aspect must appear in the relationship. The ability to plan for the future on the basis of a religious commitment to the Afrocentric worldview is the criterion of vision. Nothing can substitute for the visionary experience; it is the galvanizing element that keeps the relationship on track. To be able to ask, do you see and be assured that your partner does see the same vision provides a sense of communion. Commitment to a fundamental vision, a profound project, a spiritual quest, is the kind of commitment which demonstrates

17

vision. Relationships which are based on Afrocentric vision are never boring, dull, or without vitality. A visionary aspect to a relationship establishes a purpose outside of and beyond the daily considerations of living. The man and woman who dream together constitute the most advanced unit of an Afrocentric society.[8]

In this sense, there is much more to male/female relationships than maintaining a particular, ever elusive and precarious, standard of living.

One would be wise to consider why virtually every European story, movie, TV show, song, novel, etc., promotes a romantic love fantasy. In most psychiatric circles, the need to live in constant fantasy indicates a neurotic, if not psychotic, personality incapable of living with truth.[9] Perpetual fantasy is the world created in the mind of those in chronic denial of what they know reality is. How could any people who have done what the Europeans have done and continue to do to this planet and its people sanely live in that remembrance?

Romance is peculiar to their particular brand of insanity.

[T]o say that romance is central to all novels is to invoke a Western literary icon for other literatures. Traditionally, African writers are not concerned with the romance variety of literature...Larson is correct to see Fiedler's assertion that the "love story" is universal as another Western analysis imposed on world literature. Since there are entire cultural areas where the "love story is *non*existent, the

universality of the "love story" is doubtful.
There are no major African novels where the
plot progresses because of a hero's attempt to
attract a mate. An Afrocentric discussion of
literature would guard against this ethnocentric
promotion of a group universality.[10]

And, since it is peculiar to them, we need to understand
why this fabrication is being pushed further and further
back in human history as a means of universalizing
romance. In the truth of European culture, the history
of love is one of strict exploitation, whether of
themselves or others. It is one of the games puppets
play to the profit of puppet masters.

The problem is that we have been led to believe
that "love" occurs outside, and is completely unaffected
by, European cultural politics of exploitation. So, don't
let the spectacle of romantic love confuse you.
Europeans did not discover or invent love as they would
have us believe. Love is as old as the Afrikan. They just
turned it, as they do with everything else, into a
commodity, to be bought, sold, exploited for financial
profit.

The same mentality that started the Opium Wars
by trying to turn the Chinese into an addicted people
and went into the third leg of the "slave trade"[11] that
brought sugar from the West Indies to their homeland
for the European hordes who had been seduced into its
addiction is at work here.[12] Have we so quickly
forgotten who St. Valentine really was?[13] where Cupid
came from?[14] what chocolate does to you? whose backs
and land roses are grown on? who mines, refines and
profits from the diamonds and gold we go years into

19

irrecoverable debt to be able to give as gifts?[15]

For most players in the western mating game, it is the wrapping, not what the package contains, that initially, and often for the duration, attracts boys to girls and men to women and vice versa. True, people almost never ignore the package when choosing. That's what gets our attention in the first place. Image is everything, initially. But, one should never forget through whose eyes the package is appraised. We interpret life through the lens of the culture we are socialized in.

In Western society, selections are almost solely based on the wrappings, on social definitions of beauty, even after years of superficial conversation. Nobody says that's bad, just truth. One's exterior is supposed to reflect one's spiritual and cultural essence. But in this cultural reality a superficial and ephemeral romance concealing a constant state of antagonistic competition is the normal form that primary, intimate interpersonal interactions take. You can never reveal your true self when you are always on guard and working to gain advantage.

It is hard for those socialized in a culture that teaches all people to believe they individually and independently originate their own intelligent decisions to admit that most of their choices are not wholly their own. It is upon this ignorance that culture depends for control. The business that says that it is fully informing you because its best customers are intelligent about its products and practices is the one to be most wary of. Business thrives on ignorant and gullible customers who it can manipulate at will to purchase in excess of needs, at ridiculous prices and exorbitant interests rates. Intelligent consumers who can see through their deceit

are avoided and taken as business losses recoverable by
further exploiting ignorant ones. In all other areas,
Western culture works in the same way. And, in all
other areas as in business, conscious people cannot be
manipulated.

♒   ♒   ♒   ♒   ♒   ♒

The shamelessly demeaning picture they paint of
love and marriage in other societies is as telling as their
emphasis on romantic love. When you view the world
through glasses where others' difference is automatically
interpreted as inferior in order to establish, elevate and
maintain your interpretation of reality as the ideal model
everyone else should follow, you will lie and distort any
and every truth to create a vision of the world that fits
your reality.

> It is clear that any criticism...implies the ability
> of the critic to judge, assess, evaluate the other.
> The act of criticizing, therefore, is an act of
> imposition: One imposes one's own standards
> onto the other. In order for critical discourse to
> be effective and valuable, the recipient must
> acquiesce.[16]

For instance, what have been labeled as family
chosen marriages, including "child brides," are seen as
backward and immoral. Even though this phenomenon,
like polygamy and polyandry in traditional Afrikan
society, reflects only a small percentage of all
male/female couplings, it sets the tone for eurocentric
discussions of another culture whose civilizations and

21

society they must dismiss as inferior. Western social science is incapable of understanding the communal priority of interpersonal relationships that exists at all levels of traditional Afrikan society. Therefore, they are redefined as inhumane and anti-individual according to European cultural standards. Even if the problem of imposing European definitions on Afrikan people could be resolved by simply saying Afrikan behavior mimics European patriarchy, the reality of family on the Continent still would not compare to the depravity western men enact upon women and girls and boys in their own homes as well as around the world.

Patriarchy, in general, is defined as family and community guided by the men, usually the eldest father or collection of fathers. But western patriarchy is unique[17] in terms of the degree of dependency created for women and children and the unlimited power accorded to and exercised by males over them. In this day of the systematic political control of a fabricated humane European image, whether male or female, it is necessary to understand the tyrannical level of abuse demonstrated by European males in general at the foundational, embryonic levels of European culture.[18]

Once we visit this truth the stories advertised as news about patriarchy on the Continent will make more sense. No society's mistreatment of women and children by its men compares. The purpose and desperation behind the arrogance of the white father's, and their well schooled, colored cultural clone's, intentional misinterpretation of Afrikan family and communal structure is easily recognized when Afrika is viewed in a culturally relevant context inclusive of the historical forced infusion of European and Arab

22

realities. Today, the only real difference between the identification and official counting of acts of deviance around the world is that Europeans have cameras invading the homes of other people selectively recording what they have trained others to do but are careful to hide in themselves. Image remains everything.

It is so interesting how in these dog days of feminism and extreme individualism western scholars can only see these traditional, functioning relationships between family chosen mates, a process that for thousands of years has served to maintain group solidarity, as violating one's personal freedom, "liberal democracy," and as held together entirely by a forced subjugation of women. They must truly believe they are all knowing to assume that the few centuries of a grafted, badly plagiarized, minority "civilization" is capable of instructing and correcting scores of millennia of studied tradition. Sadly, many Afrikans agree with these children forgetting that, "Power is the ability to define reality and have other people respond to your definition as if it were their own."[19]

The very people who arrogantly feel empowered to make a judgement about another's culture, so they will be shamed into exchanging family, community and spirit for the things only extreme individualism can bring, cannot keep their own divorce rates under fifty percent. That's right. While these "backward and immoral" people have almost nonexistent divorce rates in the healthy communities that remain uninfected by European culture, over half of the people who get married in this "modern, progressive" society end up divorced.[20] And divorce rates are even higher for Afrikans here.[21] The precariousness of life in a white

23

supremacist world and the stress that it brings naturally has a greater impact on our interpersonal relationships.

This is the same loving society where most divorces are triggered by financial problems and disputes. If not beyond control already, the "cash connection"[1] becomes stronger and stronger every day as one of the most important reasons people stay together or apart. This leads us back to the question of, what's romance got to do with it if it does no more than further confuse love with sex? Understanding that culture creates thoughts and behaviors to fit its survival interests and needs, is romance the drug European culture has designed to enable two highly individualistic, selfish individuals to momentarily fixate on sex and gifts in the hope that love will somehow take over and keep them off each other's necks long enough to produce and raise their share of the next generation of highly individualistic, selfish individuals?

🐛 🐛 🐛 🐛 🐛 🐛

When the ban on interracial marriage was officially lifted with the Supreme Court's 1967 *Loving v. Virginia* decision, as if at a Kentucky derby, a line of Afrikan males raced to just fall into love with European females. Since then the numbers of males seeking mates from other groups have been highest and growing fastest for this chosen group of thoroughbreds. Many operated under the misguided assumption that racist attitudes no longer existed in the "new" liberal, progressive European mind. The decision of a high court was all the evidence needed to read acceptance into the minds of the European community.

Armchair experts on race and ethnic relations have long logically contended that racial intermixture should be considered the ultimate sign of equality. But they remain wrong in this universal, out of cultural context, thinking. They underestimate the will of and need for white supremacy in European society. The reporting and publicization of only a very small fraction of the overt manifestations of racism have reflected changes in form not content.

What has changed? Nothing has at the level of group power as a result of the initiatives of Europeans. For as Steve Biko came to teach, those seeking to change the system through working in it have not sufficiently grasped the absorptive, transforming power or necessary nature of the system. And even those who speak of changing this particular Western nation often make the mistake of assuming that "the system" is the government. Even ignoring the relationship of government to a much stronger and intricately interconnected business sector, "the system" is not the government. "The system" is the culture.

Racial oppression, or oppression period, does not require a distance between the perpetrator and victim. You can sleep every night with another you racially exploit. Males still sleep with the wives and girlfriends they physically abuse. In fact, racism works best in intimate, personally controlled environments, and even better when the victim believes the racist is not racist (i.e., the racist loves them, is doing it for their own good and they, themselves, cause the just abuse. When you get down to basics, the most enduring racist acts committed by Europeans have been covert, often in close company. They have been kept out of public sight while continuing to systematically work to maintain an extreme unequal distribution of group power. By recent example, in Azania (S. Africa) there has been no redistribution of wealth and its leaders still beg the occupying European community for fairness.[23] This exploitative imbalance no less applies to the rest of the European controlled world.

It has proven the historical prerogative of conquering Europeans to exploit the vanquished men for labor, women and children for sex and libraries for knowledge. Brutally destructive colonization is not universal among human society.[24] The ancient Ethiopians colonized the known world but not in the European sense of colonization which we have mistakenly accepted as the only definition of colonization. The Ancients infused spiritual and cultural knowledge while disseminating architectural, resource extracting and refining and agricultural technology. Once developed and mastered among the host population, the Ethiopians extracted a willing tribute from them.[25] This is not to say that there were no errors but respect was based on appreciation and awe, not fear. There is a difference between this and pillage, rape and devastation. The difference, while obvious, shows up in the contradictions inherent in the morality of white supremacy.

The "master race," then, while loudly proclaiming a strange doctrine of "racial purity" for itself, has been the world's leader in

26

bastardizing other peoples. And it has been done on a grand scale in the United States, in South America, in East and South Africa.[26]

In fact, if you are of the mentality to enslave and oppress, it makes sense to use subject populations to suit your purposes. This makes perfect sense especially if your basest sexual desires cannot be fully exploited legally at home without damaging the global projection of yourself as morally upstanding.

Using someone for sex, due to your perceptions of their sexual prowess or promiscuity or because you can't get "it" in a satisfactory amount or the way you would want it at home, does not mean that equality or freedom of choice exists for your victim.

> Rape can be consensual. Eurocentric theorists submit that that which occurred between slaves and masters, European jewish women and their Nazi tormentors, those kidnaped and their kidnappers are worthy examples of consensual rape. However, that whole discussion is irrelevant unless the European's definition of consensual is considered within the context of his overwhelming aggression as the enslaver....What Thomas Jefferson repeatedly did to Sally Hemings only has meaning within the context of a terrorizing oppression. Did she have a choice? What probably would have happened had she refused his "loving" advances. Was the probable image of her rapist as "god" a choice on her part? No matter their historian's latest lies, Thomas and Sally were not equal trading partners.[27]

27

Accordingly, the argument that interracial relationships are natural or evolutionary because guesstimates prove that a majority of Afrikans in this society already have some European blood in their veins is analogous to saying that once someone has been raped, they should continue to be raped or have indiscriminate sex because they are no longer a virgin. Such an argument is conducive to the fatalist thinking of those willing to succumb to peace at any cost. Such is fait accompli.

Webster's Ninth New Collegiate Dictionary defines fait accompli as "a thing accomplished and presumably irreversible." Thus defined, whatever is being discussed, studied, imagined or predicted is already a given fact. It is a done deal regardless of whoever or whatever may attempt to interfere with its completion. Relative to our discussion, the interracialist's argument would be that no matter the source or speed of the Afrikan-European amalgamation, it has already been initiated as a social trend which will run its natural, progressive course. Who started it, how it was started and maintained or even if it is in fact the reality presented are irrelevant questions. These questions have no bearing on the fact that it exists.

The most important insight this excuse provides into the mind of the interracialist is his/her selective denial of the relevance of historical forces. Like the relatively common yet absolutely incorrect belief that the enslavement and dehumanization of our ancestors has no meaningful impact on our current psychology, this rationalization for interracial coupling has no place for historical cause and effect.

Equal to the crime of rape itself is the

28

interpretation of the crime as a valid rationale to exacerbate it with further amalgamation. It becomes a self-fulfilling mentacide. Being polluted does not make one the pollutant.

The powerful love to play games and deal in the extremes no one else would want to or can afford to participate in. It is one of the characteristics that make them a privileged elite and separates them from those socially tracked to be "beneath" them. The exclusive claim and ability to create and control high culture distinguishes them as superior and, naturally, eccentric.

On the other hand, abused people adopt a survival or slave mentality that assumes a posture readily conforming to the wishes of any master.

> To learn to be a slave you have only to concentrate upon individual survival. You take care of yourself and yourself alone. You reduce yourself to a physical being who is determined to survive at any cost. "Take my wife and rape her, take my children and sell them, I will survive! Whip my brothers and sisters to death before me, I will survive!" This is the process by which a human being becomes a slave. [28]

However, promoting the idea that Afrikan women were generally more than willing to be sexually violated by European males and/or serve as their personal prostitutes and concubines is disrespectful at best. This betrayal at the hands of too many of their own intellectualizing sons and descendants is beyond reproach.[29] The idea of exploiting the exploitation of one's own mothers to achieve respect and fame in the

29

exploiter's ivory or ebony towers is unforgivable, no matter the quality of scholarship or praise from the European academy.[30]

In order to have a true, sympathetic understanding of the condition Afrikan women found themselves in, you would have to imagine the mentality of a people when another violently controlled every aspect of their lives.[31] You would also have to appreciate the status of Afrikan men.

For most people, the universal force of Spirit is defined as omnipresent, omniscient and omnipotent. It is everywhere. You can't hide. It knows everything. And It is the most powerful of all. Imagine how easy it would be for those whose minds went no farther than their plantation to confuse European men with Divinity. European males controlled their minds, thoughts, access to information, sleep, sexual intercourse, diet, labor, movement, etc. European males, if not everywhere, seemed to have eyes and ears everywhere. And they could punish you as if you were a child for even the most minor transgression or for nothing at all. He could, and had demonstrated he would, kill you for nothing.

If the enslaver told you to bring your daughter to his bedroom, strip her and then come back in an hour when he was finished violating her, unless you had a death wish or a plan, you did as you were told. That was not over when our physical enslavement ended. There is much discussion about what went on in this country's rural Afrikan communities, after emancipation, when the men went off to work and the European salesmen, insurance agents, bank collectors and numerous other occupational hazards became the occupying force. It was no different working in the homes of others or just walking down city streets.

> Any Black woman, practically anywhere in amerika, can tell you about being approached, propositioned, and harassed by white men. Many consider all Black women potential prostitutes. In the Village, this phenomenon was ten times worse than elsewhere. It was almost impossible to go from one corner to the next without some white man hissing at you, following you, or jingling the money in his pockets.[32]

It has not stopped today. It has only become more sophisticated.

Chapter 3. THE GREY RACE

This excuse is based on the infamous "grey race" theory. And it is the source of an old and powerful undercurrent pushing Afrikans to seek mates among Europeans. Interracial marriage, and the resulting amalgamation, is promoted as being the only means of eliminating the race problem by creating a colorless, grey race.

There are a number of fundamental problems with this line of reasoning.

(1) The percent of all married couples who are interracial is very small. It fluctuates around 1.9%. And within this minuscule proportion we must remain aware of the fact that this collection includes a significant number of couples who are not Afrikan and European.

(2) There has been a continuous decline in the percent of all married couples who are interracial.

(3) A grey race is not feasible unless made a global issue. Advocates for such a world must ask how many decades, centuries, millennia would pass before international consensus on this issue could be reached? Moreover, once decided, people would have to agree to spend their mating life continually seeking out

individuals who looked as much unlike them as possible to procreate with. Moreover, if this took place, marriage would internationally become the joke it already is in the West.

(4) Multiculturalism is a farce for those without power. One-way integration, like one-way cosmetic surgery, validates and empowers the privileged at the expense of the disadvantaged. Because European people now attempt to tap dance, jump, wear dreds (which are politically different from "locks") or become practitioners of traditional spiritual systems does not mean Afrikans have any decision making power. Such spiritless mimickings only further demonstrate their well deserved reputation for stealing and then claiming through self-righteous validation selective appearances, attitudes and behaviors that do not compromise their cultural imperatives.

Negroes and negroettes[1] are the only people on the planet crying for integration. As Chancellor Williams teaches us, integration is nothing more than "a code word for amalgamation." So whether it should even be a goal, less known a primary one, makes it highly suspect and ethically questionable. Integration is an obvious form of self-hate that feeds off of European acceptance. As Claud Anderson points out,

> Racial integration is the enemy of unity because it requires the integrating group to be subsumed, weakened and scattered as a minority in a society in which the majority rules.[2]

To which John Edgar Wideman wisely adds,

34

Integration can be interpreted as a scheme for legitimizing a form of conditional adoption.[3]

(5) Women would have to universally embrace the philosophy of producing a grey race. In order to achieve such an end without cloning and within a reasonable period of time, they would have to commit to popping out a new baby every 10 months or so for many, many, many generations.

(6) And, even if the idea of total amalgamation were universally accepted and attempted, the oppressive and divisive nature of European capitalism requires the constant creation of new forms of human exploitation for its survival. War/conflict, at all levels of society and in all forms of interaction, is a prerequisite for western profit. White supremacy will find a way to divide, segregate, antagonize and then exploit.

In the end, the lie behind this excuse is that we, here in this particular western society as leading examples of the new world order, are simply perfecting the melting pot theory. Accordingly, in the end we would supposedly become one global people, indistinguishable by color or physical features. The delusion is that we are only fulfilling some racial amalgamation prophesy. Accordingly, for those who are deceived but still question their motives out of a glimmer of historical awareness, interracial interbreeding must come to be seen as only an unavoidable biological necessity until everyone becomes visibly united as one. We feel compelled by social pressure to keep false hope alive by mentacidally believing in liberal pseudo-scientific concoctions that have no objective basis in historical fact, like races become more viable and industrious only when and if there is this crossbreeding, a misguided, wishful Darwinian thinking epitomized by the conclusions of those like Richard Poe who "scientifically" explains

> ...the phenomenon known as heterosis, or hybrid vigor. When widely different gene pools are crossed – whether among people, plants, or animals – the hybrid offspring often turn out to be healthier, stronger, larger, or otherwise better developed than either parent. Gene pools that are kept "pure," on the other hand, usually stagnate after a few generations of inbreeding into weaker and sicklier forms...The very reason that sexual coupling seems to exist among higher organisms is to ensure the maximum amount of mixing among different gene pools.[4]

Interracial marriage is a necessary legal prerequisite for miscegenation in a society that claims to respect the institution of marriage as the basis of family and child rearing. Not only that but, as stated earlier, the manufacture of a general acceptance and embracing of interracial coupling is advertised as the greatest evidence that Europeans are no longer racist. Whatever racism remaining is supposedly the dysfunctional behavior of an unenlightened minority who refuse to conform to the progressive, liberal European norm.

Maybe this reason is why most of the children of the Civil Rights Movement's leadership who supported integration have married Europeans. Apparently, that is what their parents fought for. There is no doubt that

> many black men who fought hard in the Civil
> Rights Movement were more interested in being
> able to have the White woman than in going to
> school together, eating together or riding the
> bus together.[5]

If that is your goal, your vision and interpretation of "peace, good will toward men," then that is the philosophy with which you will miseducate, disarm and disrobe your children for their enemy. And, in reference to that group of Europeans who are depicted as altruistically happening to have found their way into the hearts, pockets, votes, media imaging and voice of Afrikans but in truth selfishly extorted and wormed their way in out of full recognition that their own brothers hate them and would have them destroyed too,

> ...the jews backed and pushed the "Civil Rights"
> movement because it *helped them and kept their
> white brethren's eyes and hands off of jewish activities.*
> The mixing of the races during the "Civil
> Rights" movement and the dubious results of
> that movement benefitted the Jews and other
> whites more than Black people. It was a
> beautiful tactic and it worked. Remember, the
> lion does not sleep with the tiger even though
> they are both of the cat family.[6]

On the other hand, it might do us good to ponder why this infatuation with white skin is not the case for most of the children of the Black Power Movement's leadership.

37

☷ ☷ ☷ ☷ ☷ ☷

The natural human evolution excuse typically applies most intensely to those who voluntarily go, or are sent to places where there are no or few people of color. In these cases, proximity to Europeans is further intensified by isolation and otherwise unacceptable cultural influences.

Imagine, for example, that you find yourself living in some remote, rural hick town almost completely inhabited by Europeans. Assuming you are unable to leave, after a year or so, country and rock music may even start to sound good if they are the only sounds steadily available. Afrikans will find the beat, the rhythm. In the same way, if your hormones are ripe for sex and/or marriage, but there is nothing but European females as far as the eye can see, even they may begin to start to look good behind closed doors in the dark while blinded by the heat of physical passion. Either that or an already established preference for whiteness is given all the excuse it needs to express and fulfill itself with the locals.

This scenario about isolation and unbridled desire, however, brings another statistical question to mind having to do with Afrikan males and nonAfrikan and nonEuropean females. Since a disproportionate number of female military personnel are Afrikan, why are virtually none of them, living in and coming back from places where Asians (including Polynesians) are the majority, married to them? Skin color and hair texture are the focal points for these males who search for a mate in anything but Afrikan women. So, from the beginning, their attention has been on anything but

38

Afrikan women. The same conclusion does not apply to Afrikan men. In fact, they are disproportionately married to Asian women as compared to all racial groups of men, military or civilian. They are clearly the majority trying to produce a grey race.

Contradictions between public propaganda about interracial coupling and the statistical evidence are very valuable in revealing the politics of a culture whose scientific conclusions are based on statistics. Do your own research. When was the last time you saw a married couple where he was Asian and she was Afrikan? When was the last time you saw an Afrikan woman married to a European male living in a European slum? Compare this to the number of females clearly identifiable as "poor white trash" locked in the arms of Afrikan males in our slums.

On this planet, the worse thing that a European man can do is marry a poor Afrikan woman, no matter his class level. Afrikan women are the most disadvantaged race-gender group on Earth. And, the darker the women the greater their disadvantage. When class becomes irrelevant, when a poor European woman would marry an Afrikan male even if he were poorer, then talk to me about simply falling in love and O.J., again, or the vast majority of the males in Harvard's "colored adjunct" think tank who claim to speak for us.

> Whites do not fraternize or marry their "inferiors" unless substantial power, money or psychological benefits are derived from such a relationship. In the international arena or corporate levels you don't see any Chinese married to white people, you don't see any

Fords or Rockefellers married to Blacks because they know that *you reflect that which you sleep with* – he or she is your mirror image, is the first person you see in the morning and the last you see in the evening.[7]

In other words, perpetrators of this excuse are able but unwilling to recognize and accept the fact that

> ..."<u>INTEGRATION</u>" and "<u>AMALGAMATION OF THE RACES</u>" are in fact exercises in fatalism and wishful thinking. Why? Because there was never a time in the history of man where the slavemasters of one group ever voluntary let the other group became its equal under the same government while the slavemasters still remained in control.[8]

We need to begin asking the question of *who asks who to marry who,* and *why.* Historically, men marry "down" in terms of the education and economic assets of their brides. Afrikan men disproportionately marry Afrikan women at or below their educational and economic status. The same applies to Afrikan men who marry European women, and European men who marry European women. However, European men who marry Afrikan women are the only group who marry at their same class level or up.

Why is it that Afrikan women have to bring more than other women to the European auction block? This is an excellent, objective question, although *Essence*, the leading Afrikan women's magazine, consistently makes the mistake of failing to ask it. Of course, the degree to which this omission is truly an unintentional omission

40

must be questioned due to the magazine's increasingly European feminist, lesbian, and interracial focus. When it suggests to young, impressionable sisters to marry down or European males or pick from prison inmates, they miss the point of history, of homogamy, of why white collar Afrikan women who once married blue collar Afrikan men are no longer willing to do so. They miss the point that Afrikan women do not generally seek out the sons of Europe to marry them. They miss the point that women typically marry up, not down. But mostly, in making these suggestions to sometimes apprehensive (or unnecessarily desperate) sisters, they fail to address the question of "who asks who to marry who, and why?"

Chapter 4. A BETTER SEXUAL FIT

No, the first time I heard it, I didn't believe that some Afrikan males insisted that European and Asian women made for a better sexual fit with them than Afrikan women. But it is no longer an unusual excuse. It has gained popularity among "progressive" global culture circles. And it has become normalized by repetition. By saying and hearing it stated as fact over and over again many have come to believe it is true.

Be that as it may, whoever came up with this must have been of very limited intelligence because there is **no** scientific, biological or otherwise, evidence for this pretense. It is a desperate excuse showing the depths that negroes will stoop to camouflage their self-hate. And while we recognize that anything fitting European cultural imperatives can easily become "fact" in their think tanks and talk shows and evening news, even their science finds no correlation whatsoever between the overall physical size (height and/or weight or hand or foot size) of the participants in sexual intercourse and their physical fit, satisfaction, or anything else for that matter. No credible evidence exists relating penis size with vagina fit and/or satisfaction. Absolutely none.[1]

This excuse does make sense, however, within the European power imperative at the interpersonal level. Height and weight are directly related to power and control. The taller and larger the man relative to the woman, the more he feels like a man, the greater his self-esteem, except for those afflicted with a napoleon complex where the opposite applies.

Anthony T. Browder makes an insightful note of just how important height and race are in societal perceptions of power. He discusses a *Newsweek* photo of the stars of the movie *Jungle Fever* where Wesley Snipes, posing as in a family portrait, is positioned *below* and as in fawning submission to his European co-star Annabella Sciorra.[2] As the willing accomplice of Hollywood's drive to make him the poster boy for Afrikan males to seek nonAfrikan female mates, this familiar role is a far cry from the image Snipes attempted to impersonate in producing a video documentary of John Henrik Clarke.[3]

It is strongly and strangely reminiscent of the admittance of one who exploited being Afrikan so he could get closer to Europeans.

> Shelby Steele *boasts* of having made a bargain with himself in the early 1970s to fake Black racial identity, in order to get on with his life. Pleading the need for self-advancement, he pretended to support the cause of liberation, so as to make a way for himself.[4]

We should never overlook the personal histories of those who claimed loyalty but betrayed us in the interest of the people of their nonAfrikan spouses. There is a lesson here.

There is a reason why public figures and car salesmen tend to be taller than the average person. And it is not related to any connection between height and intelligence or skill. It is a perceptual relationship between height and intimidation.

Based on this, one is left to assume that Afrikan women are generally too tall and obese or nonanorexic to snugly fit the Afrikan male's body. European women, on the other had, are supposed to be smaller and therefore more suitable. Asian women with the smallest frames, are considered most compatible. From this, it would seem that Afrikan males using this excuse need smaller and smaller women in order to just feel like an average man. The fact that there are four times as many Afrikan males married to nonAfrikan, nonEuropean females as there are Afrikan females married to nonAfrikan, nonEuropean males attest to the small but growing number of Afrikan males who want this lie of differentiated sexual fit to be truth.

In the end, the argument is that for males and females seeking mates in this cultural wasteland, power is at the base of choice. The degree to which this is a conscious or subconscious choice is irrelevant. Consequences tell the story. Men tend to marry women who are shorter and smaller in order, in too many cases, to feel more powerful. The excessive drive to rule and exercise control over everything and everybody under every condition and in every circumstance makes this natural, even between "loving" male-female couples. Individuals socialized into Western civilization are naturally driven to seek power in all arenas.

Chapter 5. THE MATRIARCHY COMPLEX

This excuse is a product of the entrenchment of more and more Afrikans into hard core working poor, lower class and underclass ghetto slums in the late 1960s to mid 1970s. It was created out of the need of western social science to explain the extremely disproportionate and rapid increase in impoverished single female headed families. But this had to be done without attracting attention to the racist practices of a labor market that marginalized bread winning Afrikan men to peripheral, dead end jobs. The explanation had to ignore the sexist, capitalistic labor market where men formed the bedrock of stable families primarily because they had higher incomes than women. It had to blame the victim.

For this reason, the collection of single Afrikan women family heads were pejoratively labeled a matriarchy out of cultural context. Matriarchy is defined differently in the traditions of Afrikan society. Eurocentric definitions of matriarchy are

> ...unable to discern complementary relationships
> from hierarchical ones. If a family traces its
> lineage through the mother and she has power,
> then the mother must rule. They can see only

"either/or" divisions, not holistic patterns.[1]

Therefore, this scientific worldview is incapable of understanding that

> The key component of matriarchy is not that the female rules, but that the female has a principle role in culture. The male and female roles function together for the benefit of all.[2]

> [I]n the context of African cultures...[m]atriarchy denotes that kinship was determined within a matrilineal system; women had political and economic power; and motherhood had an honored and revered position. Matriarchy does not imply rule of women over men...[3]

Oba T'Shaka uses the term "twinlineal" to even more correctly conceptualize this shared, lateral distribution and exercise of wisdom and power that remains natural to men and women practicing traditional Afrikan society. He argues that

> Twinlineal is preferable to matrilineal or patrilineal, or matriarchy or patriarchy, because these terms are singular and do not reflect the Twin nature of African families. Twinlineal means that African family lineages come from the mother and the father, rather than only the mother or the father as in matrilineal and patrilineal family systems.[4]

As with all western definitions, power is the key

to deciphering the viciousness of this insult.

Eurocentrically defined, matriarchy means that women rule. They dominate all decisions affecting the group while selfishly hoarding all forms/sources of power. Accordingly, Afrikan women struggling to raise families in ghetto slums were accused of literally pushing men out of their homes. They were described as being so aggressive toward the Afrikan men who tried to live with them that they were unable to stand up and be men.

Ironically, this is the same, or similar, excuse coming to be more commonly adopted by Afrikan females seeking European male mates. The physical and verbal abuse of Afrikan males is said to drive them into the arms of the world's greatest abusers. This reminds me of the statements we still hear from sisters that only European men know how to act like gentlemen and treat them like ladies.

European males are also not oblivious to the Afrikan matriarchy stereotype. They created it. Given the portion of them who seek to be controlled and abused in sexual relations due to whatever Freudian early childhood, mother and father coveting, sexual deficit they are diagnosed by western psychiatry with, would it be stretching reason to assume that a number of those who either temporarily or permanently seek out the company of Afrikan females are searching for a woman to dominate them?

In Western culture's effort to drive a wedge further between Afrikan men and women, there is no surprise that of all excuses, the mythical Afrikan matriarchy remains the most commonly heard because Afrikan women have no real voice in mainstream middle class society. Who would listen anyway? The evidence is unquestionably stacked against them. The strongest and most telling piece is the official counts showing the lack of men in their homes.

Moreover, they have no credible defense against the accusations that they possess those qualities western culture misdefines as aggression in women. The ideal woman, who is of course European, does not exhibit these so-called uncontrollable masculine passions. Afrikan women are made strong. But the interpretation of that strength by Europeans, and negroes seeking a clear and justifiable way out of relationships with Afrikan women, demonizes this historically natural and necessary strength.

Afrikan women's spirit is necessarily forged strong, a quality misinterpreted by European society as matriarchical or aggressive. The contrast is always with their pliable, frail and dependent women who are set up as the ideal type, in a culture where there can be only one ideal type. Sisters have handled our business and rage with extreme patience and unqualified love since before we were dragged onto the shores of this Western cultural wasteland in chains and hate. What kind of disrespectful Afrikan male would buy this divisive propaganda as an excuse to slink away from the debt we will eternally owe our sisters. After 400 plus years, in this country alone, of struggling with us, watching our backs, carrying our babies and often even us, they, not us, should have the choice. As I've stated elsewhere

> the singular role of males as warriors is unAfrikan and ahistorical. Lest we forget, Queen Nzinga, Queen Judith of the Falashas,

Nefertari Aahmes, Queen Hatshepsut, and Queen Makeda of Sheba were some of our best Afrikan warriors. Black women on the Continent and throughout the diaspora remain part and parcel of the Afrikan fighting tradition. I dare you to dismiss Assata Shakur, Winnie Mandela, Ida B. Wells, Harriet Tubman, Fannie Lou Hamer or Sojourner Truth..."[5]

Something spiritual connects the Afrikan men who were consistently obstructed while attempting to fulfill the role of Afrikan manhood outside of lifting heavy objects and breeding to the Afrikan women who traditionally controlled national economies.[6] There is something beyond surviving the inhumane atrocities of the Maafa in each other's arms that connects these strong men with strong women.

Historically in this society, Afrikan women have brought home the largest share of the family income pie of any group of women. They still do. And, even though the title of having the largest proportion of their group working in the labor force was handed down to European women in 1980, they still work more hours per day, week or year than any other group of women. Sisters shouldn't have to walk around without brothers. We belong to each other.

Western patriarchy sees Afrikan women as overly aggressive toward and controlling of their men. They form a possessive western defined matriarchy, in what is supposed to be a man's domain. They refuse to accept the passive, victimized western woman's place and in doing so are faulted with creating the antagonisms that ruin the Afrikan family and community. They run their men away. They are the problem. This is how European social science normally explains why Afrikan men are not in the home and/or are setting up house with nonAfrikan women. They can't take the pressure.[7]

If you think about it though, at the same time that this excuse vilifies Afrikan women, it also says something about the strength, or rather weakness, of the Afrikan males who use the intentionally maligned, defensive and proactive posture of Afrikan women as the basis for choosing European women. For those apparently defenseless, emasculated Afrikan males, European women are seen as more desirable because they pose the least challenge to their watered down version of manhood. If just by the fact that they are not Afrikan females, European females must be naturally more permissive and passive.

Desperate contradictions reveal the truth of liars. Lies are what liars tell. And so it is here. Even now that the rate of increase in single Afrikan females heading families has stopped and reversed itself, and the rate at which white females are becoming single family heads is increasing faster than for any other group, the totally different explanations assigned Afrikan and European women as to why their men have cleared out or were never there have not changed. If anything, the lie of the Afrikan matriarchy and the fiction of European innocence have become even stronger beliefs in this culture. Through the magic of culture, myth has become reality.

Afrikan males using this excuse apparently have accepted the sexist notion that men should *control* women but don't have the guts to handle their own. They are incapable of dealing with women who have earned the right to stand up to and with them. They go out into the world systematically searching for women weak enough to sympathize with and pamper their weakened state. So the question comes down to where is their manhood? What kind of punk is driven to seek out European women he can "handle," because he has allowed other men to convince him that his own women will rule him like those men already do? The number of Afrikan males who marry Europeans using this as an excuse to find a woman weak enough to waste her time pumping up their deflated egos and failed manhood is truly amazing. Afrikan warrior scholars need the strongest women they can get their hands on to, if nothing else, skillfully handle whatever comes at their children if they themselves are wounded or fall in battle. What good would a helpless, dependent, dainty, weak skirt be to your children in a crisis of epic proportions?

Chapter 6. THE IDEAL TYPE

If you have been raised in Western society, you have been brainwashed to believe that European women are simply more beautiful than any other, even including a colored exotic discovered here or there. This "fact" is almost never openly stated but it is a subconsciously accepted truth. The confusion intentionally left by that unspoken "fact" leads many of us to believe the colorless hype, that women of all races are accepted as being equally beautiful in the so-called melting pot we live in. So, those of us who consciously recognize the truth of liars and actively promote the natural internal and external beauty of Afrikan women are accused of playing the reverse racism game. If not that, then we are said to be doing no more than trying to paint the naturally beautiful European female black.

Without fail, Afrikan apologists for white supremacy try this tactic to bring us back in line. But we have good reason to refuse their confused defenses of white beauty. Eurocentric politics have everything to do with defining European women's beauty as ideal. As with the myth of a European enlightenment before Afrikan civilization, our traditional definitions of female beauty have been corrupted and dismissed by an arrogant and purposeful European topped racial hierarchy that is compelled to define itself as the best in everything of lasting worth or admit that Europeans are ignorant and wrong about so many things. As "the claim to an absolute ultimate truth is a psychological necessity for the European mentality,"[1] Europeans know they must be seen by everybody else as *the* model of human beauty.

Someone must lead the community in asking, "What natural beauty?" Where is the beauty in an Ally McBeal or "Pretty Woman?" I don't get it. There's nothing there except jagged edges coated with pale skin. This is the beauty which we are supposed to aspire to and fall for?

Nothing there whatsoever indicates female or maternal. Things in most societies like walk or vocal pitch or hair or attire no longer generally apply to gender definitions in this so-called open-minded society. So, are we defining "nothing" as beauty. In turn, are we saying that an absence of external features or literally nothing outside necessarily indicates inner beauty? Saddest of all is that now, true to our practice of trying to be them, so many of our daughters are also striving to disappear.

How could you possibly define the media presentation of European women as the ideal beauty unless they are your daughters and you are creating and controlling those definitions? And, don't try to play on the beauty of all humans argument. We are not questioning whether or not Europeans are the crowning achievement in human beauty or barely resemble humans at all. Here and now, that question is irrelevant and distractive. The point is that this culture intentionally does not define all humans as beautiful. It cannot or white supremacy cannot prevail.

What's worse, though, is that we take their lead in our interpretations of our own beauty. Or, we will accept something which is naturally ours, such as having a behind or breasts or lips, as worthy of compliment only after they publicly admit to finding it desirable and find a way to surgically implant it onto themselves. No matter what they appropriate from others, they remain the ideal, the goal, the look and mentality to which we aspire. As a conveniently forgotten example, as soon as one of us, based on the one drop of Afrikan blood rule, was declared Miss America, we dropped the already less preferred Miss Black America from our vision of the most beautiful. No matter how sexist a circus, the Miss America and Miss Universe pageants, the *Sports Illustrated* swimsuit issues, and *Penthouse* and *Playboy*, symbolize who and what are to be judged as the most beautiful females among us, too.

Our lack of control over our images in the media is a perfect example of this. Our acceptance of any image with a declared or assumed black skin is an even better example. Close examination of every form of media from department store catalogs to the silver screen reveals a redefining, or rather more intense reviving, of what an Afrikan looks like according to what a minority of Afrikans who appear phenotypically closer to European than Afrikan. The current accelerated replacement of Afrikan males and females with biracial Afrikan-European and Afrikan-Asian offspring evinces this redefinition.

Those with an Afrikan center would ask who does

this redefinition benefit? Colorism[2] is not what is being discussed here. Afrikans are not controlling/managing the image, no matter how loudly they broadcast the incomes of a very few key exploited players. It disproportionately benefits the masters of racist culture. Others are simply pawns in their game.

> Yet we practice the European model of a racial hierarchy. And, having adopted it, any value we believe we independently, consciously or not, attach to different complexions in our community is merely a pathetic imitation of its racist beliefs at the societal level. So, in this new age of consciousness raising it must be realized that we cannot embrace a color-based hierarchy among Afrikans without, at some level, accepting as truth a hierarchy of color among humans. There is no denying that the social organization of our community along lines of color precisely mimics the order fabricated by white supremacy. Black America (Afrikans) serves as a classic microcosm in white supremacy's global macrocosm. The only appreciable difference is that we "discriminate" without power.[3]

We waste so much time seeking to retrieve or adopt those who have publicly stated they want no part of us. We even stress out trying to force remembrance into "Blacks" who prefer to be gray, European, some other nonsensical deracialized label or desperately claim to "just happen to be black." "Black people who want above all things not to be black are the most pitiable and comical people in the world."[4]

58

What is most telling about the males in this particular group is that their most often exclusive search for European women is guised in the inclusive rhetoric of "multi" this and "we're all human" that. The rhetoric is selfish, subjective and individualistic. It has nothing to do with humanity. Such an approach is incorrect. It is regressive, genocidal thinking. And, it is the classic technique of negroes, beggars and slaves, the mentality of the truly vanquished. Afrikans need to be able to identify enemies without confusion. Let those who want not to be associated with anything Afrikan go. We have too much work to do.

♉ ♉ ♉ ♉ ♉ ♉

The ecstatic adoration and praising of European male and female actors and cartoon characters as "hunks" and "babes" by live and animated Afrikan male and female performers guide the thought and opinion of viewers in our family. Since Afrikans disproportionately watch more television than any other group (over 70 hours a week on average which breaks down into over ten hours every day of the week) and this commercial medium is overly influential on the Afrikan psyche,[5] we need to be extra careful of embracing endorsements by actors who presume to speak for us but serve others. It is most interesting that only when it benefits the European image is it safe to speak of Afrikan interests and opinions as monolithic or uniform or similar.

Along these same lines, one of the main problems with books sanctioned by European publishers is in the excessively eloquent adjectives Afrikans use to describe

Europeans. Descriptions some Afrikans use to refer to Europeans such as "he was a startling, handsome blond, followed by a lovely brunette nurse."[6] and "devastatingly beautiful woman"[7] exemplify this. The point is not that they're not beautiful. That irrelevance has already been stated. The point is the lengths we go beyond what's necessary to say that they are. The instruction most of us were given about having to be two to three times as good as Europeans to just make it applies here also. In order to become successful in their fantasy world, you must express an even greater appreciation of and interest in their lives, thoughts and appearances than others, including themselves, do.

Two quotes reflecting this insanity, both out of the minds of Afrikan men, immediately come to mind.

> Out of the blackest part of my soul, across the zebra striping of my mind, surges this desire to be suddenly *white*. I wish to be acknowledged not as *black* but as *white*. Now...who but a white woman can do this for me? By loving me she proves that I am worthy of white love. I am loved like a white man. I am a white man. Her love takes me onto the noble road that leads to total realization...I marry white culture, white beauty, white whiteness. When my restless hands caress those white breasts, they grasp white civilization and dignity and make them mine.[8]

> There is no love left between a black man and a black woman. Take me for instance. I love white women and hate black women. It's just in me, so deep that I don't even try to get it out of

me any more. I'd jump over ten nigger bitches
just to get to one white woman. Ain't no such
thing as an ugly white woman. A white woman
is beautiful even if she's baldheaded and only has
one tooth...It's not just the fact that she's a
woman that I love; I love her skin, her soft,
smooth, white skin. I like to just lick her white
skin as if sweet, fresh honey flows from her
pores, and just to touch her long, soft, silky hair.
There's a softness about a white woman,
something delicate and soft inside her. But a
nigger bitch seems to be full of steel, granite-
hard and resisting, not soft and submissive like
a white woman. Ain't nothing more beautiful
than a white woman's hair being blown by the
wind. The white woman is more than a woman
to me...She's like a goddess, a symbol. My love
for her is religious and beyond fulfillment. I
worship her. I love a white woman's dirty
drawers.[9]

Another by a Afrikan woman rounds out what might
otherwise be considered a gender biased presentation.

A lot of the Black men that i met in the Village
were hung up on white women. Some of them
would come right out and tell you, "Man, i can't
dig no spade chick. Gimme an ofay every day."
When i asked them why, they said white women
are sweeter, Black women are evil; white women
are more understanding, Black women are more
demanding. One of the things that really
infuriated me was when they called Black women
sapphire. "You know how you nigga women
are, sapphire, evil." A lot of these guys would

61

have trampled over my face just to get to a white woman.[10]

Even a severely mentacidal interracialist like Calvin C. Hernton noticed this.

> However, I do not think that the personality forces that mobilize most blacks who seek relations with white women are free of ulterior or psychiatric motives. I have in mind those blacks, mostly youths, who journey from Harlem down to Greenwich Village every weekend with one purpose in mind – to "make some ofay chick." The Lower East Side of New York (the "East Village") is notorious for its interracial, bohemian-type weekend parties. White girls make themselves readily available to black boys, and black boys shuffle through the assortment of white flesh like fierce hunters on safari.[11]

This sickness, which some thought went the way of platform shoes and the Afro, never left and is now, more than ever before, becoming increasingly more normal.

The "forbidden fruit" Afrikan male interracialists seek is a misnomer except as it makes European women more appealing due to the perceived challenge of conquest. Tell these males that they can not get something, that is except empowerment for the Afrikan community, and they will "climb every mountain and swim every ocean" to get it just because. Now that addresses the "forbidden" part. But something remains dreadfully wrong with this whole concept. Fruit is supposed to be good for you. But, in this case, such a victory encourages death to Afrikans' sensibilities.

The base attraction, as so many Afrikan scholars and everyday people alike know about Afrikan male-European female liaisons, is directly tied to the sexually permissiveness or looseness of European females as compared to their Afrikan competition. What's sex got to do with it? When the body rules the head, when culture promotes its excess, when hormones kick in, everything.

> Is sex important to a Black man? Sex is the only form of gratification within reach for the economically deprived man. He cannot take a weekend cruise. He cannot hide away in his yacht at sea. He finds himself trying to crawl back into the uterus (womb) for comfort via the warm vagina. The vagina becomes the hideout for Black men seeking to escape the woes of life's challenges.[12]

On the other hand, the response to centuries of the same racist dehumanization that turned their bodies into baby factories and image into that of overly promiscuous beings has been that

> Black women are always conscious of how they are viewed when it comes to their sensuality and sexuality. Black women are least likely to report rape, as a result of the sexually promiscuous stigma. Black men view white women as easier to get sexually because they do not play the games that Black women play. Black women tend to play hard-to-get as a result of the stigmas regarding their sexual behavior. The

Black woman is least likely to be a sexual freak, because having a reputation for being moral and good is important to her. The Black woman who becomes an all-out-freak is a woman who is trying to compete with the white woman sexually in order to keep her Black man.[13]

It is worth noting the wisdom of one of our most ancient of ancestors, Ptahhotep, who said, "He who is ruled by his appetite belongs to the enemy."[14]

If beauty is not standardized according to a European model but develops out of natural, unbiased comparisons of respected differences in the physical attributes of different peoples, then why are we still looking at them to judge us?

If color and features are of no importance and preference is in no particular direction, then why does the vast majority of cosmetic surgery performed on Afrikans make them appear more European? Why the desperate emphasis on thinness; thinner noses, thinner lips, thinner thighs, thinner hips, lesser curl, lighter colored eyes?[15]

Why are our plastic and cosmetic changes only one-way? Why are these so-called cosmetic alterations almost always in the direction of the look of the ideal European? Why are we willing to accept what we naturally look like as normal and most beautiful only when we have no other choice?

Popular hair textures change. Clothes styles change. And prize winning physiques change. The only standardized facet of beauty that Europeans have consistently projected as universal is white skin. Everything else fluctuates.

Chapter 7. THE CUTTING EDGE

In an article on male-female ratios, William Darity, Jr. and Samuel Myers presented the two dominant opposing interpretations of why the already limited supply of quality Afrikan men for Afrikan women has dwindled even more.[1] One, the "alternative" perspective, blamed the institutionalized racism specifically directed against Afrikan men in the labor market for this problem. Marginalization, or being tracked out of middle to high income and prestige jobs, pushed Afrikan men to the point where many could not, with head held high, support their family, thus leaving Afrikan women to fend for themselves.

The other, an "agnostic" perspective, made the absurd argument that this society's Afrikan community had more single females heading families than others because Afrikan women were on the cutting edge of feminism. Through a convenient, but insulting, compliment, these finally intelligent women were acting on their heartfelt political beliefs that they "didn't need a man." Their choice had nothing to do with the absence of jobs, lower proportions of jobs with decent wages, or the day in, day out frustration racism brings to otherwise qualified Afrikan men. It was the logical outcome of women rejecting men in an aggressively sexist culture. It seems that Afrikan women have suddenly found themselves leading the march against the abuses of men.

As ridiculous as this explanation sounds, it still makes more sense than the fabrication that Afrikan males marry nonAfrikan females because they are at the cutting edge of social responsibility and natural humanism. It is miles ahead of any sense one can hope to salvage from the illusion that Afrikan males are leading any march into a colorless new world order.

Nonetheless, in this new humanity "we" are creating, it is a well used argument. Afrikan males who step out and ahead to lead the ragged dream of Afrikans and Europeans walking hand in hand into the future see themselves as more open-minded about human possibilities, as defined in European, i.e., universal, terms of progress. Surely we have been warned time and time again. "Do not fall asleep in your enemy's dream."[2]

This should probably be viewed as the most erroneous excuse, misinterpretating access to the sex organs of Europe's sacrificial and discarded daughters for an imagined access to the power to create a colorless Babylon. An elder sister once told me that, "a man chases a woman until she catches him." European females are far from innocent. They are as predatory as their males. Opportunity is the only distinguishing factor.

𝕴 𝕴 𝕴 𝕴 𝕴 𝕴

Given this sad state of confusion, it should come

68

as no surprise that there is no intelligent public discussion of interracial dating and marriage outside of the highly limited and extremely biased entertainment of television talk shows. Sally, Ricki, Jerry, the supermammies as well as the bald headed guy's minstrel shows excel in pushing what Kwame Agyei Akoto correctly describes as "miscegeneous homogenization."[3] Their chosen audiences exact swift punishment on those believing in a nonimperialistic pluralism where cultural integrity is defined as the ability and will of a people to maintain their distinct ethnic and biological character in the presence of other aggressively supremacist, absorbing cultures.

Sadly, but understandably, there is almost no media balance in the presentation of this issue. Advocating the dismantling of any and every vestige of the Afrikan cultural personality is clearly one-sided propaganda. If these shows, or media period, reflected western reality with any degree of truth there would have to be at least one Afrikan female coupled with a European male for every three similarly confused heterosexual Afrikan males displayed on the stage. Virtually all we see is the latter. On the popular court, relationship and family issues shows there is also an extremely disproportionate number of interracial couples, again especially of the Afrikan male-European female variety, relative to the total number of married couples.

Looking at census data for the entire population of married couples, at most, only one in every forty couples seen on these "everyday people" shows should be interracial. This falsified presentation of reality is not accidental. Producers and directors selectively

69

choose who among the numerous applicants will be actual guests. And, similarly, those wishing to be seen in the audience inquire about tickets because they agree with the political thrust. It is a self-fulfilling, self-authenticating cycle.

The intent behind this imbalanced presentation is deception. It serves no other purpose than sending another misguiding message to impressionable young Afrikan males trying to find their way in a strange, hateful European world. It is a concerted and conscious cultural conspiracy designed to encourage Afrikan males to seek out mates among European females. And, the media have been the leader in defining racial and sexual politics since European females were declared pure as the driven snow.

Do any reasonable questions remain about the true nature of the relationship between the commercial media presentation of reality and the thought and action of individuals caught up in its magic? When I was a child every boy on the block wanted to be a lawyer, doctor or international spy because that was what the idiot box told us represented success. In this day and age that conditioning has not changed. Only now sports superstars, music video superstars, gangster celebrity personalities and superpredatory law and disorder shows tell us what the present and near future labor market demands will be and who will be filling those positions.

Over most of the last two decades Afrikan male-European female couples have been paraded across our screens for the same reason. This also has been a successful brainwashing. One need only look in the malls of virtually any city as an example of the media's influence. All around, you will see very young Afrikan males escorting one or two or even more European girlfriends. As a global representation of that influence, apartheid's "official" death has issued in a mad dash by young brothers into the arms of European girls in places like Capetown, Azania.

☧ ☧ ☧ ☧ ☧ ☧

We should not require the time consuming "scientific" proof from academic camps notorious for intellectually endorsing the will of those who commit genocide against us to know that the promotion of an interracialist mentality is destroying the minds of our children. The time for studies is long over. "We know everything we need to know to teach our children. The fact that we are not doing it means we don't want to do it."⁴

Reacting to genocide and racial suicide is the mark of negroes. It is past time to act. If the media influences or largely determines clothes and language styles, musical and occupational preferences, dietary and medicinal choices, and definitions of beauty and gender roles, then why would one be naive enough to believe that the same does not apply for our racial and/or ethnic choice in mates. By now we all should know that culture is intentional.

Furthermore, what little "intelligent" discussion that does occur among that group of Afrikan males and their defenders using the excuse of being on the cutting edge of humanism sounds an awful lot like the world's largest and most privileged collection of European males crying about "reverse discrimination." It implies that somehow they are the poor, undeserving victims. It comes as no surprise that public dialogue on this issue remains closed and self-serving. Initiated and defended by the special interests of negroes who have a vested interest in preserving their own image as intelligent, thinking individuals who are acting out of their genuine concern for the good of all mankind, interracialist politics demand not only that everyone privately acknowledge this practice as appropriate but publicly embrace their sleeping with the enemy. Yet around the world

black-white mixed circles are static circles with neither direction nor programme. The same questions are asked and the same naiveté exhibited in answering them. The real concern of the group is to keep the group going rather than being useful. In this sort of set-up one sees a perfect example of what oppression has done to the blacks. They have been made to feel inferior for so long that for them it is comforting to drink tea, wine or beer with whites who seem to treat them as equals. This serves to boost up their own ego to the extent of making them feel slightly superior to those blacks who do not get similar treatment from whites. These are the sort of blacks who are a danger to the community.

Instead of directing themselves at the black brothers and looking at their common problems from a common platform they choose to sing out their lamentations to an apparently sympathetic audience that has become proficient in saying the chorus of "shame!" These dull-witted, self-centered blacks are in the ultimate

analysis as guilty of the arrest of progress as
their white friends for it is from such groups
that the theory of gradualism emanates and this
is what keeps the blacks confused and always
hoping that one day God will step down from
heaven to solve their problems. It is people
from such groups who keep on scanning the
papers daily to detect any sign of the change
they patiently await without working for.[5]

🏛 🏛 🏛 🏛 🏛 🏛

Racial politics have always been a constant in
European thought. Their immediate and future concern
over the racial distribution of social and cultural power
passes completely and undisturbed from one generation
to the next. Women have never been exempt from this
preoccupation.

In early industrializing European society when
women became the numerical majority because so many
of their men were out "discovering" the world, they
quickly became political. Powerlessly watching their
pool of quality, eligible males dwindle as more and more
went to "exploit and civilize unexplored lands and
peoples," with some even coming back married or
permanently attached to women of color, they organized
their interests and petitioned the courts. As a result,
laws were enacted making it a felony for European males
to return home married to nonEuropeans.

Based on this long forgotten litigation, and other
related events and trends since then, I would like to
suggest we consider an economic theory of interracial
mating. If not, then we need to at least seriously

consider the economic side of mate selection in a culture where an extreme individualistic capitalism rules interpersonal relationships. Alternatively, as base for an Afrikan centered analysis of this necessary connection in society, the wisdom of our ancestors knowingly defines the connection between individuals and currency in terms of cultural relations.

> An economy exists prior to money. There were economies in the world before money was invented....[A]n economic system at its base refers to the nature of the relationship between people. It's the systematic way people choose to relate one to the other that makes an economic system – Not money.[6]

And from this insight we must apprehend the fundamental mentality espoused at the level of soul by a people who have the only social order named after a thing, capital.

Marcia Guttentag and Paul F. Secord have submitted some practical observations that will further ground this economic analysis. They identified a relationship between the number of males relative to the number of females in a given group. This relationship exhibited differences in the amount of power exercised by individual males and females at the dyadic, or primary, intimate male/female couple, level as compared to the societal, or secondary, level where men associate with women in common settings.[7] And their finding, although quite simple and limited to European society, is essential to this discussion, since in human society it takes a male and a female to make a viable, complementary couple.

In attempting to explain why males have a disproportionate amount of power in dyadic relationships, they uncovered that individuals from the gender group with the least number of members will be seen as a scarce commodity by members of the other gender group. This places him or her in the position to command and, in a culture where people are seen as naturally greedy making interpersonal relationships naturally predatory, take advantage of this imbalance by exercising greater power than his/her choice mate in decisions affecting them both. Members of the minority gender can afford to be choosy because there literally are more fish in this manufactured sea ready and willing to give up more of whatever it takes to be caught. The assumptions surrounding this are elaborated in the chapter "Scarcity and Value."

This numbers game is also built into the socialization of children into functional sex-roles. Girls are taught that "falling in love" is positive and appropriate behavior while boys are taught that it is not. And this is not to say that both males and females don't fall in love in western culture. But as encoded in the sex-role socialization of a male dominated society, the person who falls in love the hardest is the one who has put her/himself in the position to be exploited the most. S/He has made her/himself more vulnerable to the approval of the other.

In a system where the exercise of power is a key component to one's self-esteem in all relationships, this emotional "co"dependency can weigh heavily on the distribution of power in dyads. And this power priority is why lying is such an important aspect of loving, intimate western relationships. It enables leverage.

Because our interest as a people centers around no less than global PanAfrikanism and because we know that we currently exist in a European style patriarchy, it is only reasonable that our interpretation of dyadic interracial relationships primarily focus on that of the Afrikan male and European female. To be effective, such a focus must tie together economic trends, male-female ratios and interracial choices.

The other half of the Guttentag and Secord argument, that the dispossessed, larger group will organize itself politically at the societal level to insure some protection and have more say in its day to day lives, completes our understanding of an economic theory of interracial relationships as it pertains to Afrikan males and European females. Unknown to most of us, currently, there is not only a shortage of Afrikan men, there is also a deficit in European men, Hispanic-Latino men, Asian men, Native American men and virtually every other kind of man in this country and on this planet. And this imbalance is exacerbated when the quality or human capital (e.g., education, income, occupational prestige, maturity, sexual preference, etc,) of males is taken into account. All males aren't men.

The current shortage in European men is no different for European women than the one they experienced during Europe's imperialistic move to colonize and enslave the world. European history shows that regardless of whether European attitudes become liberal or not, if the economy declines and a shortage of males is evident in the European population then European females become desperate. European women, who cannot find a European male as or more successful than the readily available and eager Afrikan males, become willing to *allow* Afrikan males to marry them in numbers when their personal and family survival is at stake.

That European women are culturally defined and accepted as the most desirable of all racial female groups is not irrelevant to this discussion either. As racism helps incompetent Europeans take jobs that qualified Afrikans would normally get, those European females who are at the bottom of the socioeconomic ladder or who, due to a lack of males at their socioeconomic level, exist with limited mating possibilities in an economy that takes two to tango, are rewarded just for being born white. The drive to economically provide for the survival of self and children will readily override the racist sentiment of fathers who are financially unprepared to keep their daughters racially unviolated. Choosing between no man and an Afrikan male is relatively easy for a desperate European female.

Never underestimate the importance of deceit and propaganda to the rise of global monopolization by the European community. To do so would make one nothing short of moronic. To believe that their advanced awareness of the critical shortage of males for all groups, especially their own, has not played a significant part in the interracial politics prompting a strengthening of the mixed, biracial, mulatto buffer class is to welcome one's own extinction. That Afrikan males are taking care of Europe's daughters is inseparable from this understanding. A historically grounded recognition of this should answer the question of whether Afrikan-European marriages are most influenced by more liberal attitudes among Afrikans and/or Europeans or caused by a combination of gender ratio imbalances (lack of males/females) and the state of the economy.

⚊ ⚊ ⚊ ⚊ ⚊ ⚊

Recently a student desperately but futilely tried to convince me that because his father was Afrikan and his mother European he grew up in an Afrikan and European centered home. Our confusion is truly amazing. Although the sanctioning of this confusion benefits Europeans, Afrocentrism and Eurocentrism, without apology, are incompatible.[8] They are two inconsistent interpretations of reality, history, culture and spirit which can never be bound into one. These are two different realities that, if mixed, cause insanity. Moreover, they, as cultural ideologies, are not the skin you're in. They are the mentality your skin covers.

What is scary, in relation to this student, is that, in all probability, his father was more eurocentric than his mother. Afrikan women married to Europeans tend to work to retain a larger portion of their Afrikan heritage than runaway Afrikan males. If not already perfected, the latter appear to move with all due haste to become as European as possible, with European women being little more than a means to that primary end.

Nonetheless, the problem is not with the Afrikan worldview but with the European. It is unquestionably hostile and exclusionary toward other independent worldviews. And it naturally emanates from what Amos N. Wilson describes as "White American Paranoia":

To look at the world or a segment of it with a

78

rigid, hyper-alert, and all-consuming expectation
– to search reality repetitively only for
confirmation of one's suspicions while ignoring
aspects of that reality which disconfirm those
suspicions; to pay no attention to opposing
rational arguments, cogent, well-founded
evidence, except to find in them only those
features that seem to confirm one's original
views; to examine reality with extraordinary
prejudice, rejecting facts, information and
alternative possibilities while seizing on and
exaggerating any scintilla of often irrelevant
evidence that supports one's original
expectations – denotes a driven need: a
psychoneurotic, psychopathological need to
defend an ego perilously in danger of
disintegration and to defend it regardless of cost
to oneself and others. Such a suspicious and
paranoid orientation speaks to the need to
rigidly construct and control reality so as to
maintain self-control, to empower the ego and
to gainfully exploit a relevant situation.[9]

This is not a truth about which we should get lost in
mindless, redundant, divisive, distracting debate.
Eurocentrism is about maintaining white supremacy and
further positioning Afrikans against each other while
removing the Ancients as a force in our thoughts.
Afrocentrism is designed to bring Afrikans together, to
reconnect us with our Way. Becoming Afrikan centered
takes us even further to the level of nationbuilding.

But, in line with this new age miseducation about
race and culture, what we increasingly encounter are
thoroughly confused students who want to hold on to
some facet or trinket or symbol of the Afrikan tradition

because it is in vogue, yet remain safe within their European privilege. They have not bridged thought to action. And, in turn, they are more afraid of Afrikans than Europeans.

This particular student had been well trained. Of critical importance to him, and individuals like him still unwillingly trapped "behind the veil" of their skin, is gaining some semblance of integratedness, of being equally a part of the powers that be. In this effort, they assist the white supremacist agenda by seeking to control language and redefining what is Afrikan to suit their European mind.

Since so many of these lost souls must look like and live among Afrikans, they have to rationalize the insanity that comes from wanting to be European, or at least accepted by them. The problem is not Afrikan acceptance since we will accept anybody thrust upon us, even those fanatically in denial of being Afrikan. The problem is that this Afrikan-European group wishes to remain in both worlds, just in case.

It is incredible how the propagators of European culture conveniently redefine the Afrikan to suit their agenda. That is exactly what they did and are still doing to classical Afrikan civilization. When they cannot dismiss original Afrikan thought, behavior or material technological mastery, they systematically deny that Afrikan centered thought and behavior and European centered thought and behavior are different or incompatible. It is all simply reduced to *human* thought with *them* being the defining universal ideal. As a result of internalizing this nonsense, we find a large collection of confused "Afrikan-Europeans" who, while not necessarily the product of Afrikan and European parenting, believe that they can sport a dashiki, some kente cloth, a kofi, dreds or an ankh while praising and promoting European individualism and expressing patriotism to western society.

There is no doubt that Europeans adapted Afrikan culture without acquiring most of the knowledge or taking it through the appropriate stages of development. They remain unable to handle Afrikan culture properly with its inextricable spiritual quintessence. An enormous amount of time is required to adapt and develop organic civilization as compared to the short time one needs to adopt and develop mechanical technology. We are erroneously and ahistorically operating on the unavoidable progression principle that European culture is the natural culmination of the best that human culture has to offer. Little could be further from the truth. European culture hindered, arrested or destroyed every culture it encountered. It was a process of destruction and pillage not contribution or improvement through infusion.[10]

Chapter 8. SCARCITY AND VALUE

It is also widely believed that universal law governs interracial mating. Supposedly, a rule beyond the power of human refusal draws Afrikan males to European females. Afrikan males chase them for the same reason we are told diamonds carry a higher price tag than other precious gems. They are rare. And, when matched with desire, scarcity naturally increases value. Robert Staples is but one scholar who sought to write this misinterpretation of value and desire into reality as if European cultural politics were not intricately involved. He is convinced that:

> Certain factors seem almost universal in determining physical attractiveness....One is the rarity of a physical trait in its most exacting form. The more abundant a trait is, the less it tends to be highly regarded. Another is Whiteness. Even in predominantly White cultures, blondes are the preferred coloration.[1]

Putting that into the statistics of race and gender, because European women make up less than 6% of this world's women they can be considered rare. Devoted interracialists work hard to make this analogy of diamonds to European women a valid comparison. Minority status is said to necessarily make them more valued and sought after as mates than women from more populous groups, than women who just happen to be of color. European women's novelty cannot help but make them the most desirable. It's only natural.

Because of the generalized equation of scarcity with increased worth, this excuse has been defended as originating outside the diseased womb of western cultural politics. Like arguments of genetic intellectual inferiority or superiority, these relationships are claimed to be beyond any individual fault or ulterior motivation on the part of the males or females involved. They are simply operating in accordance with the laws of nature.

Yet, one question should pique our curiosity about just how apolitical this argument really is. If this attraction based on scarcity/rarity is a naturally occurring phenomenon, then why don't the statistics fit the human reality? Why does this logic not apply in this society or the European fatherland where European women constitute the largest group of women? Here and there European females are more sought out by more males who don't look like their brothers than females from any other group. Yet the converse does not obtain even though Afrikan women are a clear minority here and there.

Are we to assume that Afrikan males in European strongholds like this society, the Netherlands, Germany, England and Australia have miraculously shed their miseducation and developed a more informed awareness that somehow enables them to calculate the global presence of various "types" of women and intelligently choose the least populous and therefore most precious, thereby enhancing their social portfolios? That is quite doubtful even through a great stretch of the imagination.

It would not take a psychiatric study to show that many Afrikan males conspire with the enemy within to create the illusion of digging up white diamonds in the Afrikan community by transplanting European women there. The rationale behind the plot thickens when these thoughts are devised in this country where European females constitute well over 30%, or the majority of any single group of women, of the population.

Disempowered Afrikan males so desperately want to believe such an acquisition will dramatically increase the value of their holdings and, in turn, enhance their social standing. The belief that European women, rare or plentiful, short or tall, attractive or homely, big or small, blond or brunette, smart or dumb, add value to and enhance the prestige of these males is common knowledge.

The magnitude of this mentacide is further evidenced by the fact that once a European female is planted in the Afrikan community, she never has to worry about her or her children's security as compared to Afrikan women and their children. If one Afrikan male discards her, there is another impatiently waiting in the wings to take up the slack. Without question, we will harbor them.

The problems historically associated with the thinking of this select group of enterprising males are well known in the Afrikan community. We are not fooled. The only fools are those who feel that this excuse will deceive anyone outside themselves. Afrikan male lust for European women requires no rationalization. So why give it? Lack of skin color is the single most important attraction to vanquished males of color in white supremacist society where whiteness holds the highest single value. The personality, intelligence, femininity, sexual agility/capacity or other qualities that may accompany it are simply icing on an already angelic cake.

Globally, people with color almost instinctively gravitate toward Europeans. It has nothing to do with numbers. It has everything to do with power and the persistence and proficiency at which Europeans go about the business of invading the space of others and forcefully defining reality for them in the European image. It has everything to do with how they insidiously weave themselves into the center of everyone else's reality. The idea of accessing power and validation by kissing the oppressor's feet, whether there is one pair or millions, or by touching the hem of his daughters' skirts, is not new. Dependent thinking people invariably seek out others who will "feed them." Ayi Kwei Armah captures this mentality for us in his dramatization of the thoughts of a seasoned negro.

> Once we agree to work for the whites, we put ourselves on the road to power. It is a road without end...If we help the whites get this control, we stand to profit from the changes. Those foolish enough to go against them will of course be wiped out. I'm among those who'd

rather profit than be wiped out....Nothing will
ever make me stand against those guns. The
only place for me is firmly by the side of
whoever possesses such powerful weapons....[I]n
this world there are those who thrive, and there
are those who don't. Those who thrive, thrive
because they respect power. They see where it
comes from, and they take care to place
themselves beside it, never against it.[2]

In this cultural environment, no European will
ever be alone or without admirers seeking to suck up
their political amorality and intellectual trivia. As
extensions of a homage demanding white supremacy,
admiration by others becomes a naturally occurring
method for building up their self-esteem.[3] Any lie
supported by "universal" law, no matter how politically
manipulated or farfetched, will do in the race of others
to sit at European feet and provide for and protect their
children.

Chapter 9. THE BIG PAYBACK

In retaliation for the years of enslavement, lynching, castration, dismemberment, dehumanization and emasculation,[1] Afrikan males seek to hit the master where it hurts most. We want to recoup our losses, in the form of their most valued and sacred property. We want to possess and freely violate their daughters. Only then would individual justice be exacted.

It would, of course make more sense, in a capitalist system where the monopolization of wealth is the foremost key to their power, to hit them in the pocket. There is nothing between their daughters' legs that can empower anyone in the Afrikan community. The terror invoked by even the possibility of having to confront other men is the mark of vanquished males. So, given access and opportunity, many Afrikan males strike where they are allowed, "like a blind man with a pistol."[2] These guerilla warriors hit and run under the covers in darkness.

The refusal to stand against men as men is also a refusal found among some of our more vocal would-be revolutionaries. Eldridge Cleaver is one of the better known leaders of this romanticized, "ofay" stomping brigade. Whether consciously or not, each rationalizes a string of European female lovers as a means of getting back at their master, the European man. The energy expended developing and rationalizing the psychosis individuals generate within when they are driven to work through a compromised but potentially cathartic revenge is insightful.

> I became a rapist....I started out by practicing on black girls in the ghetto...and when I considered myself smooth enough, I crossed the tracks and sought out white prey...Rape was an insurrectionary act. It delighted me that I was defying and trampling upon the white man's law, upon his system of values, and that I was defiling his women – and this point, I believe, was the most satisfying to me because I was very resentful of the historical fact of how the white man has used the black woman.[3]

One cannot help but wonder how much the Afrikan male's addiction to "angel dust" or "snow queens" hurts the dealers of European power. Moreover, "practicing on black girls" would seem to contradict an Afrikan man's anger over how "the white man used the black woman." Even if by some impossible feat of the Afrikan imagination, rape was made appropriate, he would still be venting in the wrong direction.

Nonetheless, as counterrevolutionary as sleeping with the enemy is, it seems that a number of the so-called revolutionary elite do feel the need to pay back the European forefathers in this fashion. Although the payback theme isn't always openly stated, this tendency largely characterizes members of the revolutionary leadership class. However, it would be unfair to single them out because their only advantage is in opportunity, which may be the deciding factor relative to the rank and file membership. Nonetheless, the excuse seems to rear its pitiful head during peak reactive periods when "revolutionaries" strive to be their revolutionary best. Claudia Jones speaks to this mentality as normal behavior in the Communist Party, once considered the most liberal European organization accepting and using Afrikans.

> Some of the crassest expressions of chauvinism are to be found at social affairs, where, all too often, white men and women and Negro men participate in dancing, but Negro women are neglected.[4]

This excuse, like the others, is not limited to males. Today, there are many feminist who just happen to be Afrikan. Feminism however, as a European phenomenon, needs to be compared to Womanism, a Afrikan choice. As noted by Afrikan women warrior scholars, feminism must be understood as the effort of European women to take the power from European men so they can become the privileged exploiters. In contrast, Womanism is an effort on the part of Afrikan women to gain full respect from Afrikan men in our fight for the empowerment of our people.

Be that as it may, the fact remains that many of the most visible and successful "Black feminists" model this seemingly proud tradition of sleeping with an enemy of the same gender, rationalizing their "marriage" through the ulterior politics of a feminist-Marxist-interracialism. They, too, seek to kick the "white man" below the belt.

Yet in heterosexual interracial relationships, no group of women are more guilty of complicity than European women. There is no doubt that they thoroughly enjoy the doting attention they receive from Afrikan males. If for no other reason than of the temporary yet extreme rebellion characteristic of youth socialized in western culture, taking an Afrikan lover is about the worst retaliation a daughter of the master race can inflict on her parents. It should go without saying that the flood of solicitations from Afrikan males makes it easy for European females to discreetly, legitimately and innocently satisfy their curiosity about the Mandingo mystique.

But to return to the male perpetrators, someone needs to clarify just how protecting and providing for another's daughters, leaving all your assets upon death to them and neglecting sisters hurts "whitey." There has been no redistribution of power as a result of this self-serving insanity. If anything, there has been the greater consolidation of it in the hands of the European community. In fact, this excuse sounds more like a childish "I'll fix you" threat.

Who is really giving payback here? Who is really being raped? Who is still on top of the Afrikan male who is fighting to get on top of the European female? In his desperate fight for survival at the top, the European male is not above using his women to undermine his enemy's warrior class males. This applies whether his women are aware of their exploitation for their cause or not.

In the final analysis, finding a scapegoat to mask an absence of manhood is characteristic of boys, not men. In war, men don't substitute caring for their enemy's daughters with confronting that enemy. This makes about as much sense as going home and committing the treason of beating up on the sister who loves you because you are not man enough to take control of your destiny and stand up to the man creating your frustration, even if that means losing your job and having to build your own. Again, the weakness of this excuse arises in the inability of those Afrikan males to get at the master. "For the master's tools will never dismantle the master's house."[5]

Chapter 10. PROXIMITY

People tend to date and marry others at the same social and economic class level. This speaks to the concept of homogamy we briefly defined in the introductory chapter. This truism is strengthened by the fact that people also tend to rape, rob and kill those living near them, who also tend to be at the same social and economic class level. The increased mobility afforded youth by the debt producing purchase of private transportation on credit might appear to have the potential to significantly alter this historical universal. But as of this point in time it hasn't. This society's youth still disproportionately date and marry people in their own neighborhood or community. Whether attending college or working, people prefer to mate with and/or marry someone who also goes or works there.

These facts, however, form the base of another erroneous defense proposed by self-interested Afrikan males. This time they insist that they marry European women because they happen to find themselves sitting next to them in class. They claim to naturally follow the social pattern of marrying those females who they find spatially closest to them.

Yes, most of us are miseducated in predominantly European educational institutions in college and at the graduate and professional school levels. And, yes, most interracial coupling occurs in college. But with closer examination, the "I couldn't find any qualified Afrikan women around" excuse sounds a little too much like the usual European employer's excuse of never being quite able to find a qualified Afrikan in a sea of us, or like that of too many of our predominantly Afrikan colleges that hire additional European philosophy teachers in already all European departments because they can't seem to locate an Afrikan philosopher, again, when a more than ample pool is eligible and available.

This is an important point because philosophy is the base of the social sciences and the eurocentric philosophy teachers in front of our sons and daughters are still teaching that philosophy, or rational thinking, originated in Greece, a lie thoroughly debunked by George G.M. James[1] and supported by the work of many, many others including Cheikh Anta Diop,[2] Henry Olela[3] and Drusilla D. Houston,[4] to name but a few. The sad thing is not that these departments refuse to hire Afrikan philosophy teachers but that they continue to undermine the historically correct, self-awareness of Afrikan students at historically Afrikan populated colleges and universities by reinforcing the lie that philosophy began in Greece, not Afrika and, that even if it were somehow partially true that philosophy began or reached its apex on the Continent, students could still read the Greeks and get what the Afrikans said and understood. The faculty in these departments either argue that scholars addressing the Afrikan origins of human philosophy like Cheikh Anta Diop, George G.M. James, Jacob A. Carruthers, Theophile Obenga, John G. Jackson and Yosef A.A. ben-Jochannan are "not real scholars" or that they are not important in the academy because they were not required to read them. Eurocentrists could not continue doing this to our children unless we still reinforced our children's belief that Europeans are omniscient.

Be that as it may, since most interracial marriages do occur among those who meet at the same college, this excuse would seem to hold some water. Again, most of us who go to college attend majority European institutions of higher miseducation. But, still, something is tragically flawed with the logic. It just does not fit the numbers. And we know that if the statistics don't fit the stated theory in the West we can't have scientific fact.[5]

First, there are over six college educated Afrikan women for every one college educated Afrikan man. Such a disparity clearly indicates a wealth of highly mobile and available, "quality" Afrikan women for college educated Afrikan men. And, as this evidence of an excess of qualified Afrikan women applies for college interns and graduate and professional school students and graduates also, the proximity excuse used by Afrikan males in the public and corporate sectors deserves to be held in the same contempt and dismissed accordingly.

If anything, the ratio of 32 employed or in school Afrikan males of marriageable age to every 100 Afrikan females of marriageable age should void any and all excuses alleging a shortage of quality Afrikan women.[6] Yet even this 32 is still a dangerous overcount of available Afrikan males. There is no discussion of how many in this group are open or closet homosexuals[7] or have chosen to exclusively or disproportionately date and marry nonAfrikan females. The significant number of males choosing to remain single are also not calculated. All of these groups would inadvertently remain in the official statistical pool of available Afrikan males.

Second, the statistics do not support the supposedly "distressing" nature of this choice expressed by some Afrikan males who seek public sympathy for their choice of mate. Confessions of inescapably finding themselves surrounded by European females on historically European college and university campuses and finally submitting to that game is supposed to evoke a sympathy similar to that given those coming out of the proverbial Western closet. Even though already proven with official statistics showing that there are more Afrikan women than Afrikan men in college, common sense would tell us that there are many more Afrikan women than Afrikan men attending European colleges. If the laws of proximity and homogamy hold, then we should expect to find many more Afrikan women who discovered themselves seated beside European males now married to them than Afrikan males to European females.

The actual ratio of three Afrikan males married to European females for every one Afrikan female married to a European male tells us something else is in operation. Even though there are four times as many Afrikan males married to nonEuropean, nonAfrikan women as Afrikan females with similar spouses, "the number of Black men that are married to European women far out-number any and all other cross-culture

98

marriages."[8]

Chapter 11. A PARENT'S LOVE

Although technically not an excuse, one reason that it is a factor in interracial relationships is the way parents raise their children. The excuse of being guided by their parent's love usually isn't given by Afrikan males as a reason for single-mindedly focusing on European females as partners. More often than not, neither the parent nor child is able or willing to explain how or why cultural tastes are transmitted from parent to child through normal child rearing.

Nonetheless, a parent's love is seen in the development and expression of the child as s/he comes to maturely interpret and interact with this world and the people and things in it. More than anything else, such concern helps fashion the mentality that naturally develops consciously and subconsciously in the child's mind as s/he searches to find his/her own way of looking at the world. In the formative stages of childhood, this mentality is naturally patterned after that of the parents, assuming they are the true first teachers and primary caregivers.

But that's only one aspect of this process. For out of their experiences, beliefs, aspirations and fears for themselves, parents subjectively and selectively interpret the world in a particular way and seek to influence the worldview of their children in that direction. Parents give their children what they believe will protect and gratify them as they grow up in whatever reality they believe their children do and will live in. Yet, because of its lack of articulation, this explanation appears as more of an innocent reason than excuse because blame tends not to be leveled at caring parents or their impressionable children. No matter, a justifiable rationale is implied.

While probably the least recognized excuse, the guiding example of racial pride or disdain parents set tends to be extremely influential in the conscious and subliminal choices Afrikan males make in considering who they marry and/or who the mother of their children could be. This excuse is virtually a silent killer of young developing Afrikan spirits. It is the only one in this collection of excuses that directly points to the irresponsible choices made by responsible parents as a significant contribution to racial genocide. It works in two related ways.

First, it actually condones European mates for Afrikan males through an unqualified "we're all human" logic. It was W.E.B. DuBois who again tried to warn parents against raising our children to reach for the stars without teaching them about the reality of white supremacy.[1] He realized that it is better for them to know of racism and never encounter it than to not know and be knocked off balance or devastated by its first occurrence. Racism depends on the shock of unexpected physical and psychological terrorism to keep its victims off balance and confused.

> We must also teach our children that to be pro-black is not to be anti-white – one of the greatest farces perpetrated on the mind of black folk ever. We must teach them to continuously recognize all manifestations of racism. Since when is blame and recognition synonymous? Since when does the recognition of a cause automatically enable that cause to become a disabling handicap in one's effort toward achieving an end that in and of itself will reduce that problem and its perpetrators to meaninglessness?[2]

Historically disconnected messages of colorless humanity endorse and insure the production of young Afrikan males whose neutered aggression makes them tame enough for society to not need to control them as they grow into adulthood. Again, the common bond of humanity logic, once taken out of historical, cultural and political context, plays a pivotal role in these formative lessons. Through them one becomes as good or bad as his/her enemies, even if they are killing you. The sins of one become the sins of all.

And taming Afrikan males, in preparing them to be assimilated through external approval, satisfies the other way this excuse fulfills its rationalizing mission. It induces Afrikan minds to believe they are the initiators of the European's will. Through this process they are made ready for European women to use to experience their fantasies about the Afrikan man's sexual prowess in their journey to become the women of the world that their men already herald themselves as being. This is done while Afrikan males also serve the function of taking up the slack of the European male shortage.

The motive for rearing extraordinarily nonaggressive males originates from historical remembrance. No matter how we try to suppress it, or feign denial, Afrikan parents remember the history of their conquest. It is genetically encoded culturally. It has been embedded in our living collective consciousness through two thousand plus years of psychological assault.[3]

> Not only has the mental and physical hostility directed toward the Afrikans in this hemisphere been consistent and pervasive up until the present, but distorted realities caused by the chronic trauma of The Maafa have resulted in behavioral changes and distortions. These behavioral changes and distortions, which have gone without treatment or recovery since the initial traumatic inflictions, have become the learned behaviors of generation after generation. Therefore, we have a complex reality in which chronic trauma and distorted realities have been passed through generations as learned behavior, while increasing distortions are heaped upon the Afrikan existence by the continuous nature of chronic trauma.[4]

As a universally stated principle in the psychology discipline relating historical awareness to contemporary thought and action:

> Simply because we choose to forget a traumatic event, simply because we choose not to learn of a traumatic history and a history that may make

us feel ashamed, does not mean that that history is not controlling our behavior. Simply because we don't know our history, and may have not heard of it, does not mean that the history does not control our behavior.

One of the most profound things that we've learned in psychology is that the most powerful forces that shape human behavior are those factors that are consciously *not* remembered by human beings, are those experiences the individual can swear he's never had. That is one of the paradoxes of human behavior, that the very things that shape us and make us behave the way we do, see the world the way we see it and relate to people the way we relate to them, are those things that occurred in our lives at points we cannot remember or recall.[5]

Any time we may choose to forget our responsibility to instill acceptable levels of subservience in our children this society is more than willing to remind us.

Afrikan parents know who they are dealing with. That's why we lie to our children in the name of protecting them. Such excuses are shameless. We are not protecting them. We are trying to protect ourselves from the pain we know will come to them and us if they stand up.

No matter how we try to play it off, we understand that Europeans will kill them in a second, for nothing. We understand that our sons are looked upon as the greatest threat to European hegemony for good reason. And yes, as men, they are our last line of defense. There is nothing unrealistic about these fears.

They are reasonable for a people who subconsciously understand the nature of their oppressor, as evidenced in historical fact, yet feel powerless to confront it.

However, these reasonable fears lead to insanity when they cause us to believe that no matter what we do the European will rule forever. "Oppression does not destroy a people. It is the acceptance of oppression that destroys."[6] Our actions become divorced from our words. We consistently compromise our stated power and morality. By example, we subconsciously establish limits for our children at the same time that we tell them they are limitless. By following the example set by their parents, emasculated Afrikan males become living expressions of confused, powerless mentacidal negroes.

To ensure the safety of their children Afrikan parents know they must make integration and absorption, a foremost priority. It becomes more and more urgent that they be spread out among our enemy. And in doing so we must make them believe that it is their responsibility to make a color-laden world colorless.

Palestinians once hid their European-Israeli hostages throughout their cities in the hope that the knowledge that they would kill one or two of their own would deter Western missiles. Like Afrikan parents, they misunderstood European's sense of martyrdom. Racial nationalism has always overridden any appreciation of life in European culture. Any notion of sparing an innocent's life has never stopped them from sacrificing their own.[7]

Yet this mentality is not incompatible with encouraging interracial dating and marriage.

106

A Parent's Love

Nonwhite people don't understand the necessity for white supremacy domination, but white people understand that they have to dominate. So when a white person is in bed with a nonwhite person, because of the long history of conditioning that tells them nonwhites are inferior, the nonwhite person will be programmed to love white people...The highest desire, under white supremacy programming, is to be loved by a white and validated by a white person. So the white person who is acting counter to white genetic survival by engaging in sexual activity with the nonwhite person is actually achieving a greater goal: the goal of domination. The nonwhite person's mind has been turned against their own interest...the nonwhite person has to turn against the interests of other nonwhite persons to protect the interests of the white person they're in bed with. That means the white person is the dominant person, no matter who's on top or bottom in the act of sexual intercourse.[8]

She is far from alone in her deduction. In his discussion of *The Insane Nigger* Mack B. Morant concurs with this when stating that

...any black person who buys into an inter-racial marriage can in no way stand up and support the black race completely. He or she will compensate psychological or physical defense mechanisms to protect his or her white wife or husband and in many ways shield their own conscience.[9]

Plus, it emasculates potential Afrikan warriors. Interracial marriage and statements of colorlessness are based on the desire to become indistinguishable from the master and get as far away from the Afrika we still hate and are embarrassed by as we possibly can, except in misguided efforts to go back and economically and religiously exploit it as new world colored carpetbaggers. Afrikan males exhibiting the least aggression against European cultural imperialism are increasingly rewarded with superficial tidbits of success. The marriage and care of a European girl shows her father that her negro is safe and worthy of larger crumbs. Negroes must successfully pass every proctology exam in order to move to the head of the class.

$$\text{\Large ⚒ \quad ⚒ \quad ⚒ \quad ⚒ \quad ⚒ \quad ⚒}$$

A concern for his children's future also leads Afrikan males to seek out European spouses. Mulatto, or biracial, children remain the recipients of greater privilege for obvious historical reasons. It has been successfully argued that they are aesthetically more pleasing to the eyes and sensibilities of Europeans. Western society's distaste yet fondness for the products of Afrikan-European unions has never changed. Look at the history.[22] Or, just turn on the TV. Who disproportionately stars in "Black" female leads? Are such truths painful? Yes, but we have no more time to mourn the tragic mulatto than the poor little rich white girl.

In whatever country on whatever continent you look, after the people from the Caucasus Mountains ravage and appropriate their civilization, you see the proliferation of children produced by Caucasians raping conquered women and girls. The majority of these offspring, siding with their most powerful parent, come to form a buffer class between paranoid European elites and terrorized dark hordes. Because of their dual racial citizenship, mulattoes have historically been favored as agents of "crowd control" over the darker masses. Many scholars make note of this phenomenon in the history of European global imperialism.

If history is a tool for learning so that mistakes are not repeated, and if we are wise enough to discern events repeating themselves over and over again forming patterns to our disadvantage, then we must understand the connection between a developing privileged mulatto class to the maintenance and strengthening of white supremacy. Chancellor Williams detailed this pattern in his *The Destruction of Black Civilization.* But, regardless of the qualifying recognition that should be given to those mulattoes who understood and understand who their people are, his point taken out of early Egyptian history has remained a constant that deserves our undivided attention here and now.

> The end result was always the same: The Blacks were pushed to the bottom of the social, economic and political ladder whenever and wherever the Asians and their mulatto offsprings gained control. This scheme of weakening the Blacks by turning their half-white brothers against them cannot be overemphasized because it began in the early times and it became the universal practice of whites, and is still one of the cornerstones in the edifice of white power.[11]

The bastardization of a people is a basic European divide and conquer strategy. It enables the absentee ownership of people through the biological creation of a home grown marginal elite intensely loyal to their fathers. We find this as a pattern throughout the world Europeans have violated and laid claim to. Scholarly examinations of some better known examples of the mulatto nationalism handcrafted by the intentional cultural politics of European imperialism can be found in the interactions of the Blacks, Coloreds, Indians and whites of Azania[12] and the international descriptions given by John Henrik Clarke,[13] Chancellor Williams,[14] Randall Robinson[15] and Jacob Carruthers.[16]

This evidence in no way condemns all or even most of those who had no choice in being born of two races. House slaves caught hell, too. Nor, for that matter, is it an attempt to confer on all relatively "pure" Afrikans an Afrikan nationalistic loyalty. There is no doubt that negroes contaminate the range of our complexion. However, Williams' suggestion that those mulattoes who remained loyal to their Afrikan heritage should be praised, singling them out for "special honor,"[17] as compared to Afrikans born without the privilege of choice, is a questionable recommendation.

Skin tone is one of the least important indicators of who is or is not Afrikan.[18] Clarence Thomas, Vernon Jordan and Armstrong Williams are perfect examples of this misconception. Afrikanity is a mentality. It is an identification with a revolutionary Afrikan history, present and future. It is mental.

Those who *will* to work for justice and who understand that work as their conscious responsibility will be found in all places and in all walks of life, at all levels of formal education and at all income levels. There are no class divisions nor language barriers for those who do this cosmic work.[19]

Afrikan consciousness covers the range of complexion in our community. It does not discriminate based on pigment. "We are Africans not because we are born in Africa, but because Africa is born in us."[20]

From this brief look at a historical pattern it would not take a leap in thinking to conclude that Europeans today, well aware that their time is up, are doing everything in their power to enlarge and further strengthen the buffer class they hope will serve to protect them from a forgiving but unforgetting and furious dispossessed people.[21] A racially indistinct buffer class serves to confuse, misdirect and dissipate this justifiable rage. When operating as a political unit in the service of European culture, such a buffer class escalates racial confusion among Afrikans. The mulattoization of a significant segment of the world's Afrikan population through the biological and surgical infusion of Europeanized features will seriously confuse and compromise racial origins, responsibilities and global politics.

As already stated, this fact is not new in the minds of Europeans sitting precariously on their throne of enforced racial privilege. Their media, and the individuals selected as spokespersons in that fantasy, reflect this awareness. Because of their high visibility, statements about their race by popularized individuals such as Tiger Woods and Mariah Carey, who in their confused yearning to identify themselves as "American" attempt to claim every possible European strain as part of their racial makeup, and consistently identifying these minority genes first, promote the spread of the racial confusion which sustains the internal chaos necessary for the voluntary maintenance of white supremacy among the darkest populations.

A contemporary movement illustrating that this treachery has not ceased is rising among those wanting to be categorized outside of Black or white census categories. Multiple/biracial census categories serve the interests of those who wish to have the socially accepted right to claim nonloyalty to Afrikans, those who may appear but don't want to be Afrikan, and those who seek to separate and elevate themselves in the tradition of their historical mentors who selfishly lapped up their share of the material and social spoilage as privileged members of a buffer class. No matter the publicity stating that this move is to establish themselves apart from Afrikan and European as the "New Americans," the new colorless human race, these group politics serve a purpose. Their mission is informed by both history and the rapidly unfolding social devastation. Be not deceived, the purpose is not to get closer to the powerless. It is to move deeper into the house of the European who remains entrenched at the top of the human food chain.

But is our thinking too small, not grand enough for the challenge? Can we see through the European vision of unlimited power and control into the future? Have they now moved beyond manipulating nations to a final, total, conquest and domination of a so-called global culture? The new world order is original

European imperialistic thinking. It is not new. So, since nothing has changed there, and the world has grown significantly smaller, are they now trying to create and consolidate a buffer race to control the world's people of color? Have individual nations been no more than haphazard experiments leading up to this final test?

☘ ☘ ☘ ☘ ☘ ☘

It's amazing, but not surprising, that people pointed out and publicly discussed every major point Andrew Hacker made in *Two Nations* except one. Somehow they forgot a major detail guiding his thesis. He had no question that many Europeans already recognize that their time is up.

> Liberals also hold a theory about the sweep and tenor of human history. While seldom stated as a coherent philosophy, its premises occasionally become explicit. One such tenet is that the era of white dominance is coming to an end. If nothing else, birthrates dictate that the approaching century will belong to people of color, just as immigration is changing the texture of the United States. True, the Western world still has military might; but it lacks social goals and moral purpose. Hence the desire of liberals to find a place for themselves in the new era: so the future will note that they were among the few white persons who foresaw what was coming and were prepared to accept their diminished status.[22]

This is the basis of European politics, of white

supremacy – the drive to racially survive.

🪳 🪳 🪳 🪳 🪳 🪳

Speaking of community and family, the reason for the absence of any fear whatsoever by Europeans of Afrikans retaliating against them for marrying into the Afrikan community is easily answered.

> ...why aren't the Black man and White woman accepted by the White nation? The answer is simple. The White nation forbids its members from acting in certain ways and have sanctions to back up its demands. But when it comes to the Black nation it is thought to be some kind of political child sucking on the breast of Good Public Opinion, unable to demand anything less it be labeled selfish, racist, inconsiderate of the needs of others...This kind of plight of the Black nation has caused both the Black man and the White woman to expect the Black nation to accept their union as being holy and to entrust them with the most critical missions.[23]

And, based on this reality,

> The reason that whether Black men marry White women and whether Black women marry White men is a problem in the first place, is that Black people act powerless and exert powerlessness. For if we were not powerless we would just simply set up certain guidelines concerning marriage and those individuals bucking our will would get fucked and that would be all to it.[24]

114

"Successful" Afrikans living among Europeans are able to transcend and dismiss the approval or disapproval of the Afrikan community because their income and validation are derived from elsewhere. Likewise, Afrikan businesses, social and cultural organizations, schools and churches that are subsidized by the European community have nothing to stop them from changing their loyalty, if there is ever any desire to do so.

At the other extreme, by infusing Afrikan families and individuals into European communities you make it easier to systematically commit cultural and physical genocide without anyone pointing the finger at you. Proximity makes it easier to pollute Afrikan culture and monitor and manipulate the Afrikan status quo. By allowing "others" into their neighborhood no one would think to blame their crimes on racism. The Columbine High School murder of a completely innocent Afrikan male is yet another tragic example of this. The commission of genocide against Afrikans, and every other people of color, in their midst has never ceased. It has only again become more visible.

The wisdom that "What goes around comes around" and of "chickens coming home to roost"[25] is again being confirmed. The outward spread of the European disease of chaos with their invasion of the planet prevented a terminal implosion then, but they will never be able to escape universal law. It has returned to its maker with a vengeance unheard of in human history. And it cannot be stopped because it has manifested itself in their seed, their children. Before, they were able to establish the lie that chaos was the product of a disadvantaged subculture of poverty that Afrikans could only blame themselves for being disproportionately imprisoned in. The chaotic state of Afrikans, considered to be naturally disempowered and intellectual and moral inferiors, was said to be a quality uniquely found in their genetic predisposition for deviance.

Time brings truth. And now even their own media can no longer contain their naturally disruptive spirit. Western media are a product of European culture. And as such, in the same way that European children learn the benefits of turning on their parents, Western producers and directors have found a way to profit from exploiting their own children.

What has forced the public unveiling of their well concealed natural social state is the increasing, unpredictable and unstoppable explosion of "death, destruction and domination" in their communities at the hands of their own children. Two important reasons inside an aggressive and antagonistic cultural base inform this. One, the spoiling of their children has reached the point where parents cannot control their access to destructive technology (music, cable, movies, chemicals, explosives, weaponry, etc.). And, two, a multinational political economy which has no concern for the jobs of European youth, has facilitated the relocation of jobs outside western nations and encouraged and allowed the invasion of domestic labor markets by less demanding and more loyal nonEuropeans.

The logic behind why European workers in this society have not yet seriously revolted against their elite is well explained by Clarence Munford's version of the "surplus value" theory. European-to-European loyalty is based on even the least among them being only relatively deprived as compared to Afrikans. No matter how bad the economic situation, their incomes and wealth (access to loans, investment opportunities, grace periods, etc.) remain higher than their Afrikan contemporaries.[26] Even "Appalachian whites," considered by far the lowest on the European economic totem pole, can rest easy knowing that at least they were not Afrikan.

☧ ☧ ☧ ☧ ☧ ☧

Mentacidal Afrikan males, unable to face the reality of their master's impending fall, seek to produce children who will have the best of chances in what they conceive of as the everlasting European world order. Believing that the diminished white presence in this society's population signals that Europeans do need the negro,[27] they jockey to reserve the more opportune positions closer to the master for their children. Also, while realizing that Europeans cannot produce color, they recognize that they must mate with Europeans in order to immediately, significantly and, hopefully, permanently lighten their descendants. They seek to have their children granted most favored status by their oppressor.

The practice of Afrikans "passing" for Europeans is well documented. Historical and especially contemporary evidence clearly show that this social psychological drive exists and is still being passed down into the minds of our children as a viable option among some Afrikans.

As of the year 1950, the defectors had soared to

12,000 per annum. By 1980 the yearly tally was 17,000. If that number held steady during the 1980s – conceivably it was greater – then during that decade alone, some 170,000 persons abandoned Black identity and the Black American community. Even a conservative estimate would place those who slipped away to pass for white in the sixty years from 1930 to 1990, at some 630,000.[28]

Furthermore, we have readily adopted the euphemism of "crossover" as a popular expression to make the possibilities less remote and the personal and public betrayal less painful.

No matter how one looks at this excuse in its entirety, it clearly indicates that there is an understanding of European racism, even if only in the form of a defeated attitude toward challenging it. Afrikan males who marry interracially refuse to shoulder their responsibility to the women and families in their community and choose to believe that racial hierarchies are natural and indicated by divine blessing. Since God rewards his chosen, European people must be the most favored people or they would not be in charge. "White men have ruled over us for so long, to some it seems like one of the physical laws of nature."[29]

Chapter 12. CONCLUSION

"Powerlessness breeds a race of beggars."[1] A successfully oppressed people desperately seek the love of their oppressors for self-validation. They are subconsciously, mentacidally driven to culturally assimilate in an effort to compel their oppressors to accept as a moral obligation the burden of stopping themselves from further mentally, physically and socially destroying their victims. Cultural and spiritual assimilation is irrelevant in that they have already put forth every possible effort to divest any resemblance of the traditions of their ancestors from themselves. When that does not work, when they come to realize that white supremacy cannot exist without racism, when it finally clicks that sharing is not on the European agenda, when they finally realize that "it's not what you say that they don't like, it's you they don't like",[2] then the final stage of integration must be entered.

When skin color and phenotypical differences are the visibly distinguishing features of oppressor and oppressed, then amalgamation, or the permanent removal of visible racial differences by sexually producing a less and less distinct racial population, becomes the primary goal of the survival oriented among the oppressed. It's that simple. One need only skim a short list of some well known Afrikans who were or are sleeping with Europeans. We would be remiss if we did not include Ira Aldridge, Maya Angelou, Kofi Annan, Pearl Baily, Amiri Baraka, Charles Barkley, Harry Belafonte, Julian Bond, Ed Bradley, Carol Mosely Braun, Lonnie Bristow, Avery Brooks, Georg Sanford Brown, Clarence Williams III, Johnetta Cole, Ward Connerly, Sammy Davis, Jr., Father Divine, Frederick Douglass, Marian Wright Edelman, Olaudah Equiano (aka Gustavus Vasa), Franz Fanon, Roberta Flack, Henry Louis Gates, Clarence Gilyard, Cuba Gooding, Jr., Berry Gordy, Dorien Harewood, Ken Hamblin, Calvin Hernton, Chester Himes, Gregory Hines, Michael Jackson, LaToya Jackson, Reggie Jackson, C.L.R. James, Rick James, Jack Johnson, James Earl Jones, Quincy Jones, Vernon Jordan, Monica Kaufman, Eartha Kitt, Earl Klugh, Ramsey Lewis, Wynton Marsalis, Ali Mazrui, James McDaniel, Bobby McFerrin, Barbara McNair, Edwin Moses, Thurmond Munson, George Padmore, Clarence Page, Floyd Patterson, Scottie Pippen, Sidney Portier, Richard Pryor, Lou Rawls, Alphonso Ribiera, Dennis Rodman, J.A. Rogers, Roxie Roker, Diana Ross, Richard Roundtree, Leopold S. Senghor, O.J. Simpson, Mike Singletary, Kristoff St. John, Shelby Steele, Clarence Thomas, Melvin Van Peeples, Ben Vereen, Alice Walker, Hershel Walker, Walter White, Charles V. Willie, Montel Williams, Fred Williamson, Richard Wright, and William Julius Wilson.

The point of presenting these excuses is not to initiate or engage a great debate. As previously stated, we need not waste our time with intentional, irrelevant distractions. This was written so that people, especially Afrikan males, can feel free to stop fooling only themselves with these fabrications, stories and lies. Humanism has nothing to do with it. Be men. Tell the truth. Stand firmly behind your contradiction. The only remaining question is, "Why do these diseducated negroes and lost souls feel it so necessary to continue to manufacture erroneous, ungrounded explanations, unsupported even by the science of their masters, ad nauseam, to those who should care less why they are sleeping with the enemy?"

ENDNOTES

1. Garry Pierre-Pierre, "The White Wife," *Essence*, July 1998, pp. 80-82 and 138-139.

2. He coined this term in an essay entitled "Mentacide: The Ultimate Threat to the Black Race."

3. Trenton, NJ: Africa World Press, 1992.

4. *Enemies: The Clash of Races*, Chicago: Third World Press, 1978, p.186.

5. The original and perpetuating causes of this escalating process as well as historical descriptions of this phenomenon are found in the writings of Margaret C. Simms and Julianne M. Malveaux (eds.), *Slipping Through the Cracks: The Status of Black Women*, New Brunswick, NJ: Transaction, Inc., 1986, William J. Wilson, *The Declining Significance of Race*, Chicago: University of Chicago Press, 1980 (2e), William J. Wilson, *The Truly Disadvantaged*, Chicago: University of Chicago Press, 1987 and Andrew Hacker, *Two Nations*, NY: Charles Scribner's Sons, 1992.

6. Sam Roberts, "Pay Gains by Black Female Grads May Be Discouraging Marriage," *Atlanta Constitution*, October 31, 1994.

7. Larry D. Crawford, "The Cultural Continuum," *Frontline*, Vol.2, No.12, December 1998, p.16.

8. Stokely Carmichael (Kwame Toure), "Pan-Africanism – Land and Power," *The Black Scholar*, Vol.1, No.1, November 1969, pp.37-38.

9. Trenton, NJ: Africa World Press, 1991.

10. Trenton, NJ: Africa World Press, 1994.

11. Bronx, NY: Afrikan World InfoSystems, 1993.

12. Washington, DC:)yoko InfoCom Inc, 1999.

13. Tallahassee, FL: Nubian Nation Publications, 1992.

14. Chicago: Third World Press, 1999.

15. Columbia, MD: Kujichagulia Press, 1995.

16. *Osiris Rising*, Popenguine, Senegal: Per Ankh, 1995, p.102.

17. John Henrik Clarke, *African World Revolution*, p.341.

18. Carruthers, *Intellectual Warfare*, pp.140-141.

19. *The Maafa & Beyond*, p.105.

Chapter 2

1. Los Angeles: Middle Passage Press, 1994, p.91.

2. San Francisco: The Black Scholar Press, 1982, p.129.

3. His books *The Five Negro Presidents*, St. Petersburg. FL: Helga M. Rogers, 1965, *Nature Knows No Color-Line*, St. Petersburg. FL: Helga M. Rogers, 1952, and *Sex and Race, Vols. I, II and III*, St. Petersburg. FL: Helga M. Rogers, 1944 endeavor to reconstruct a pattern to this.

4. Sterling Plumpp, *Black Rituals*, Chicago: Third World Press, 1972, p.93.

5. How well we imitate European's redefinition and abuse of love is deeply considered in Nathan Hare and Julia Hare's *Crisis in Black Sexual Politics* (San Francisco: Black Think Tank, 1989), Haki Madhubuti's *Black Men* (Chicago: Third World Press, 1990) and Delores P. Aldridge's *Focusing: Black Male-Female Relationships* (Chicago: Third World Press, 1991).

6. However, one could start with Ra Un Nefer Amen, *An Afrocentric Guide To A Spiritual Union*, Bronx, NY: Khamit Corporation, 1992, Sobonfu Somé, *The Spirit of Intimacy*, NY: William Morrow and Company, Inc., 1999, pp.1-131 and Kwame Agyei and Akua Nson Akoto, *The Sankofa Movement: ReAfrikanization and the Reality of War*, Washington, DC:)yoko InfoCom Inc., 1999, pp.117-128.

7. Kwame Agyei Akoto, *Nationbuilding: Theory & Practice in Afrikan Centered Education*, Washington, DC: Pan Afrikan World Institute, 1992, p.9.

8. Molefi K. Asante, *Afrocentricity*, Trenton, NJ: Africa World Press, 1988, pp.52 and 54.

9. For a basic definition see Philip G. Zimbardo and Floyd L. Ruch, *Psychology and Life* (9E), Glenview, IL: Scott, Foresman and Company, 1975, pp.484-485. For the application of this definition to Europeans and negro apologists see Bobby E. Wright, *The Psychopathic Racial Personality*, Chicago: Third World Press, 1984, pp.1-15.

10. Molefi K. Asante, *The Afrocentric Idea*, Philadelphia, PA: Temple University Press, 1987, pp.6-7.

11. We would do well to view this as a misnomer. For a credible path to understanding, read Erriel D. Roberson's *The Maafa & Beyond* (Columbia, MD: Kujichagulia Press, 1995).

12. Eric Williams provides indisputable documentation of this created addiction in *Capitalism and Slavery* (Chapel Hill, NC: University of North Carolina Press, 1994 (first published 1944)).

13. Marcus 3X, "Who Was Saint Valentine?," *Unpublished Paper*, 1997.

14. Marcus 3X, "Who Was Cupid?," *Unpublished Paper*, 1997.

15. Insightful indicators can be found in Joel Kotkin, *Tribes*, NY: Random House, 1992, pp.52-58 and Cheikh Anta Diop, *Black Africa: The Economic and Cultural Basis for a Federated State*, Chicago: Lawrence Hill Books, 1987. And, as intricately related to this on the general issue of relative consumption at the group level, read Claud Anderson, *Black Labor, White Wealth*, Edgewood, MD: Duncan & Duncan, Inc., 1994, E. Franklin Frazier, *Black Bourgeoisie*, NY: Collier, 1962, Nathan Hare, *The Black Anglo-Saxons* (2e), Chicago: Third World Press, 1991, Melvin L. Oliver and Thomas M. Shapiro, *Black Wealth/White Wealth: A New Perspective on Racial Inequality*, NY: Routledge, 1995 and Larry D. Crawford "Black Capital," *Frontline*, Vol.II, No.XII, August/September 1997, pp.13-18.

16. Asante, *The Afrocentric Idea*, p.26.

17. Excluding some Asian nations, particularly Japan.

18. For a sample of what evolved between then and now see pages 16-19 of my "The Cultural Continuum." *Frontline*, Vol.2, No.12, December 1998.

19. Wade Nobles, *Africanity and the Black Family*, Oakland, CA: Black Family Institute Publications, 1985, p.107.

20. Rodney Stark, *Sociology* (4e), Belmont, CA: Wadsworth Publishing Company, 1992, pp.389-390.

21. M. Belinda Tucker and Claudia Mitchell-Kernan, "Trends in African American Family Formation: A Theoretical and Statistical Overview," in M. Belinda Tucker and Claudia Mitchell-Kernan (eds.), *The Decline in Marriage Among African Americans*, 1995, p.10 and Shirley Hatchett, Joseph Veroff and Elizabeth Douvan, "Marital Instability Among Black and White Couples in Early Marriage," in M. Belinda Tucker and Claudia Mitchell-Kernan (eds.), *The Decline in Marriage Among African Americans*, 1995, p.177.

22. Maulana Karenga listed four "connections" that worked to the disadvantage of male/female relationships in western culture. Besides cash there are the "flesh," "force" and "dependency" connections (*Introduction to Black Studies*, Los Angeles: Kawaida Publications, 1982, pp.214-219).

23. As John Henrik Clarke foretold and we can see even more clearly what happened here happen there with the arrival and entrenchment of other Europeans and their negro carpetbaggers,

> If the whites in South Africa eliminated apartheid tomorrow, the Africans would still be in difficulty because they would have no economic power and their

land would still be in the hands of foreigners. (*Notes for An African World Revolution*, Trenton, NJ: Africa World Press, 1991, p.384)

24. Michael Bradley, *The Iceman Inheritance*, NY: Kayode Publications Ltd., 1991 (first published 1978), pp.162-163, Chcikh Anta Diop, *The Cultural Unity of Black Africa*, London: Karnak House, 1989 and Chancellor Williams, *The Destruction of Black Civilization*, Chicago: Third World Press, 1987, p.283.

25. Drusilla Houston, *Wonderful Ethiopians of the Ancient Cushite Empire*, Baltimore, MD: Black Classic Press, 1985 (first published 1926), George G.M. James, *Stolen Legacy*, Newport News, VA: United Brothers Communications Systems, 1989 (first published 1954), pp.9-11 and, although still feeling compelled to find a way to eurocentrize, i.e., make tyrannical, these preEuropean relations, Richard Poe, *Black Spark, White Fire*, Rocklin, CA: Prima Publishing, 1997, pp.161-166.

26. Williams, *The Destruction of Black Civilization*, p.74.

27. "Racism, Colorism and Power," *Frontline*, Vol. 3, No. 7, October 1999.

28. Albert B. Cleage, Jr., *Black Christian Nationalism*, Detroit: Luxor Publishers of the Pan-African Orthodox Christian Church, 1987 (first published 1972), p.9. More specifically, Haki Madhubuti outlines the survival mentality (*Black Men: Obsolete, Single, Dangerous?*, Chicago: Third World Press, 1990, pp.7-10) while Na'im Akbar speaks to that of the slave mentality (*Chains and Images of Psychological Slavery*, Jersey City, NJ: New Mind Productions, 1984).

29. E. Franklin Frazier, *The Negro Family in the United States*, Chicago: University of Chicago, 1966 (first published 1939), pp.50 and 53-69, Rogers, *Sex and Race, Vols.II and III*, and Rogers, *Nature Knows No Color-Line*.

30. Although it can have its benefits. Frazier became the first Afrikan to be elected (by an almost all European collection of colleagues) as president of the American Sociological Association. Afrikan firsts, as accomplished in European culture, are not always things to celebrate. That William J. Wilson was the second and only other Afrikan to fill this prestigious position is a statement in and of itself. Europeans have never rewarded anyone who seriously called them into question.

31. See Akbar, *Chains and Images*, pp.21 and 42-58.

32. Assata Shakur, *Assata*, London: Lawrence Hill Books, 1987, p.106.

Chapter 3

1. In the context of my discussion, the label negro

> ...marks those among us who grow from our knees; those
> of us who believe that crawling is fine as long as they get
> the biggest crumbs. Or as Kelly Miller says, "The negro
> pays for what he wants and begs for what he needs." The
> question should not be, "Shouldn't you crawl before you
> walk?" Instead, the question is, "How long must you
> crawl before you walk like a man?" How long must four
> appendages be your mode of transportation before you
> recognize that two will more efficiently and effectively do
> the job? (Larry D. Crawford, "I Am Not Ashamed,"
> *World African Net Website*, August 1998)

2. Claud Anderson, *Black Labor, White Wealth*, Edgewood, MD: Duncan & Duncan, Inc, 1994, p.187.

3. John E. Wideman, *Fatheralong*, NY: Pantheon Books, 1994, p.74.

4. *Black Spark, White Fire*, Rocklin, CA: Prima Publishing, 1997, p.500.

5. Rosie Milligan, *Why Black Men Choose White Women*, Los Angeles: Milligan Books, 1998, p.118.

6. Haki R. Madhubuti, *Enemies: The Clash of Races*, Chicago: Third World Press, 1978, p.187.

7. Ibid, p.188.

8. Yosef A.A. ben-Jochannan, *Africa: Mother of Western Civilization*, Baltimore: Black Classic Press, 1988 (first published 1971), p.87.

Chapter 4

1. Herant A. Katchadourian and Donald T. Lunde, *Fundamentals of Human Sexuality*, NY: Holt, 1972, p.26 and W.H. Masters and V.E. Johnson, "Ten Sex Myths Exploded," in Nat Lerhman, *Masters and Johnson Explained*, Rockville Centre, NY: Playboy Paperbacks, 1970, pp.231-232. No research since these "scientific" studies of the "sex revolution" has contradicted this natural, species maintaining, fact.

2. *Survival Strategies for Africans in America*, Washington, DC: The Institute of Karmic Guidance, Inc., 1996, pp.25-26. These are only two of the key points he makes in discussing this relationship.

3. *John Henrik Clarke: A Great and Mighty Walk*

4. Clarence Munford, *Race and Reparations*, Trenton, NJ: Africa World Press, 1996 p.314.

Chapter 5

1. Miriam Ma'at-Ka-Re Monges, *Kush, The Jewel of Nubia: Reconnecting The Root System of African Civilization*, Trenton, NJ: Africa World Press, 1997, p.129.

2. Ibid, p.129.

3. Ibid, p.152.

4. *Return To The African Mother Principle of Male and Female Equality, Vol I*, Oakland, CA: Pan Afrikan Publishers and Distributors, 1995, p.XII.

5. "Voices in the Tradition of the Afrikan Warrior," *World African Net Website*, October 1998.

6. Cheikh Anta Diop, *The Cultural Unity of Black Africa*, London: Karnak House, 1989, Charles S. Finch III, *Echoes of the Old Darkland*, Decatur, GA: Khenti, Inc., 1993, pp.77-78, Ife Jogunosimi, "The Role of Royal Women in Ancient Egypt," in Maulana Karenga and Jacob Carruthers (eds.), *Kemet and the African Worldview*, Los Angeles: University of Sankore Press, 1986, pp.31-42 and Monges, *Kush, The Jewel of Nubia*, pp.125-153.

7. Although Oscar Lewis (best known for his *Children of Sanchez*, NY: Vintage Books, 1963) initiated this contemporary discussion of women's behaviors and attitudes in "cultures of poverty," it was Daniel P. Moynihan's *The Negro Family: The Case for National Action*, (Washington, D.C.: U.S. Government Printing Office, 1965) that promoted a racist slant in public policy decisions that was directed specifically at Afrikans in this society. His findings were further "objectified" by the observations of mainstream ethnographers like Elliot Liebow (*Tally's Corner*, Boston: Little, Brown, 1967), Lee Rainwater (*Behind Ghetto Walls*, Hawthorne, NY: Aldine Publishing Company, 1970) and Ulf Hannerz (*Soulside*,

NY: Columbia University Press, 1969). Scholars like Douglas G. Glasgow (*The Black Underclass*, NY: Vintage Books: 1981) and William Ryan (*Blaming the Victim*, NY: Pantheon Books, 1971) tried to correct this cultural misinterpretation only to encounter the usual limited success that humane oriented social issues experience during economic downturns in capitalist systems.

Chapter 6

1. Marimba Ani, *Yurugu: An African-Centered Critique of European Cultural Thought and Behavior*, Trenton, NJ: Africa World Press, 1994, p.23.

2. This is more extensively discussed in my "Racism, Colorism and Power," *Frontline,* Vol. 3, No. 7, October 1999.

3. Ibid, p.1.

4. Gwendolyn Brooks

5. Also see Anthony T. Browder, *From The Browder File*, DC: The Institute of Karmic Guidance, 1989, pp.47-50.

6. Ossie Davis and Ruby Dee, *With Ossie and Ruby*, NY: William Morrow and Company, Inc., 1998, p.189.

7. Calvin C. Hernton, *Sex and Racism in America*, NY: Anchor Books, 1988 (first published 1965), p.28.

8. Franz Fanon, *Black Skin, White Masks*, NY: Grove Weidenfeld, 1967, p.63.

9. Eldridge Cleaver, *Soul on Ice*, NY: Dell Publishing Co., Inc., 1968, p.159. The reader is encouraged to read his entire "The Allegory of the Black Eunuchs" starting on page 155. Sometimes confusion in one serves to manifest clarity in another.

10. Assata Shakur, *Assata*, London: Lawrence Hill Books, 1987, p.112.

11. *Sex and Racism in America*, p.75.

12. Rosie Milligan, *Why Black Men Choose White Women*, Los Angeles: Milligan Books, 1998, p.48.

13. Ibid., p.78.

14. In Asa G. Hilliard, Larry Williams and Nia Damali (eds.), *The Teachings of Ptahhotep*, Atlanta: Blackwood Press, 1987, p.23.

15. Crawford, "Colorism, Racism and Power, p.18.

Chapter 7

1. "Sex Ratios, Marriageability, and the Marginalization of Black Males," *Challenge*, 3 (1992): 5-13.

2. John E. Wideman, *The Cattle Killing*, NY: Houghton Mifflin Company, 1996, p.146.

3. *Nationbuilding: Theory & Practice in Afrikan Centered Education*, Washington, DC: Pan Afrikan World Institute, 1992, p.8.

4. Ronald Edmonds as quoted by Barbara A. Sizemore in Kwaku Person-Lynn, *First Word*, NY: Harlem River Press, 1996, p.191.

5. Steve Biko, *I Write What I Like*, London: The Bowerdean Press, 1996 (first published 1978), pp.23-24.

6. Amos N. Wilson, *The Falsification of Afrikan Consciousness: Eurocentric History, Psychiatry and the Politics of White Supremacy*, Bronx, NY: Afrikan World InfoSystems, 1993, pp.44-45.

7. *Too Many Women? The Sex Ratio Question*, Beverly Hills: Sage, 1983.

8. See Kwame Nantambu, *Egypt & Afrocentric Geopolitics: Essays on European Supremacy*, Kent, OH: Imhotep Publishing Company, 1996, pp.37-50 and Tony Martin, *The Jewish Onslaught*, Dover, MA: The Majority Press, 1993, pp.51-66.

9. *Black-on-Black Violence: The Psychodynamics of Black Self-Annihilation in Service of White Domination*, Brooklyn, NY: Afrikan World InfoSystems, 1990, p.37.

10. Ra Un Nefer Amen makes the elemental statement (*Metu Neter, Vol I.*, Brooklyn, NY: Khamit Corp., 1990, pp.23-25). A

immeasurably small sampling of the evidence of the massive destruction Europe's expansive war machine wrought on human civilization can be found in Lee Miller, *From the Heart*, NY: Alfred A. Knopf, Inc., 1995, Erriel Roberson, *The Maafa & Beyond*, Columbia, MD: Kujichagulia Press, 1995, pp.15-27 and Chancellor Williams, *The Destruction of Black Civilization: Great Issues of a Race From 4500 B.C. to 2000 A.D.*, Chicago: Third World Press, 1987. And, also providing the theoretical basis for the cultural logic informing the European mentality behind their attitude and behavior toward "others," see Marimba Ani, *Yurugu: An African-Centered Critique of European Cultural Thought and Behavior*, Trenton, NJ: Africa World Press, 1994, p.409-485.

Chapter 8

1. "Beauty and the Beast: The Role of Physical Attraction in the Black Community," in Nathan Hare and Julia Hare, *Crisis in Black Sexual Politics*, San Francisco, CA: Black Think Tank, 1989, p.70.

2. *The Healers*, London: Heinemann, 1978, pp.30-32.

3. See Paulo Freire, *Pedagogy of the Oppressed*, NY: Continuum, 1996 (first published 1970) and Albert Memmi, *The Colonizer and the Colonized*, Boston: Beacon Press, 1965 (first published 1957) for analyses of the love and admiration engendered through oppression for the oppressor.

Chapter 9

1. A sampling can be found in Ida B. Wells, *A Red Record: Tabulated Statistics and Alleged Causes of Lynchings in the United States, 1892-1893-1894*, Chicago: Donohue & Henneberry, Ralph Ginzberg, *100 Years of Lynching*, Baltimore, MD: Black Classic Press, 1988 (first published 1962), Stewart E. Tolnay and E.M. Beck, *A Festival of Violence*, Chicago: University of Illinois Press, 1995, Wintrop D. Jordan, *The White Man's Burden*, NY: Oxford University Press, 1974, pp.81-83, Thomas F. Gossett, *Race: The History of an Idea in America*, NY: Schocken Books, 1965, pp.269-273 and Del Jones, *The Black Holocaust: Global Genocide*, Philadelphia: Hikeka Press, 1992.

2. Chester Himes

3. Eldridge Cleaver, *Soul on Ice*, NY: Delta, 1968, p.14. Near the bottom of the same page he refers to a similar quote from Amira Baraka's (LeRoi Jones') work. The scale of this frenzy is dramatized in the rest of Calvin C. Hernton's statement about the interracial games played three decades ago in Greenwich Village of the 1960s in *Sex and Racism in America*.

> As one goes from party to party, from one beatnik bar to the other, one becomes aware of a kind of mutual conspiracy between white women and black men. One of the features that characterizes the behavior of these blacks is their attempt to intimidate the white male by making free play with his woman. (NY: Anchor Books, 1988 (first published 1965), p.75)

4. Tony Martin's introduction to C.L.R. James, *A History of Negro Revolt*, Chicago: Research Associates School Times Publications, 1994 (4th ed), p.ix.

5. Audre Lorde, "The Master's Tools Will Never Dismantle the Master's House," *Sister Outsider*, NY: The Cross Press, 1984,

p.112.

Chapter 10

1. *Stolen Legacy*, Newport News, VA: United Brothers Communications Systems, 1989 (first published 1954).

2. *The African Origin of Civilization*, Westport, CN: Lawrence Hill & Company, 1974 (first published 1955).

3. "The African Foundations of Greek Philosophy," in Emmanual Chukwudi Eze (ed.), *African Philosophy*, Malden, MA: Blackwell Publishers, 1998, pp.43-49.

4. *Wonderful Ethiopians of the Ancient Cushite Empire*, Baltimore, MD: Black Classic Press, 1985 (first published 1926).

5. This, of course, applies to all but *eureason*, the articulated logic of the European worldview, where "theories are more precious to some scholars than facts, even when the facts flatly contradict their theories" (John G. Jackson, *Ethiopia and the Origin of Civilization*, Baltimore, MD: Black Classic Press, (first published 1939), p.10).

6. Darity and Myers have presented the findings of major research from 1985 data on the Afrikan male shortage from the most generous to most conservative ("Sex Ratios, Marriageability, and the Marginalization of Black Males" 1992). The ratios which ranged from "1) the ratio of men to women of marriageable age (14 years of age and older) [to] 2) the ratio of unmarried males to unmarried females [to] 3) the...ratio of employed males to females [to their own] 4) the ratio of unmarried males in the labor force or in school to unmarried females" found 73:100, 48:100, 46:100 and 32:100, respectively. Darity and Myers' comparison of the rapidly decreasing percentage of available Afrikan males according to all the studies they looked at from 1976 to 1985 say much about where the ratios probably sit now.

7. Guesstimates about the size of this group among Afrikan males fluctuates around a "strong (and growing) six percent" (Sylvia

Perry, "Through Thick & Thin: An Open Letter to Black Males," *The Atlanta Voice*, April 6, 1998, p.5).

8. Rosie Milligan, *Why Black Men Choose White Women*, Los Angeles: Milligan Books, 1998, p.105-106.

Chapter 11

1. *Darkwater: Voices From Within the Veil*, NY: AMS Press, 1969 (first published 1920), pp.203-204.

2. Larry D. Crawford, "I Am Not Ashamed," *World African Net Website*, August 1998.

3. Three masterpieces demonstrating this are Na'im Akbar's, *Chains and Images of Psychological Slavery*, Jersey City, NJ: New Mind Productions, 1984, Amos N. Wilsons', *The Falsification of Afrikan Consciousness: Eurocentric History, Psychiatry and the Politics of White Supremacy*, Bronx, NY: Afrikan World InfoSystems, 1993 and Carter G. Woodson's, *The Miseducation of the Negro*, Trenton, NJ: Africa World Press, 1990 (first published 1933).

4. Erriel D. Roberson (Kofi Addae), *Reality Revolution*, Columbia, MD: Kujichagulia Press, 1996, p.124.

5. Wilson, *The Falsification of Afrikan Consciousness*, p.34.

6. Albert B. Cleage, Jr.

7. An example worthy of consideration is the sacrificing of their own in order to get at four brothers trying to break out of a court house at the height of the country's assault on the Black Panther Party. George Jackson's brother Jonathan

> [h]ad passed out automatic pistols to the inmates at the hearing who joined him: Arthur Christmas, Ruchell Magee and James McClain. A shotgun had been tied to the neck of the judge. The prosecutor, selected members of the jury, and the judge had been marched outside at gunpoint....They had marched outside to a van, all hostages, and entered the van. Then the bullets had rained down. Hundreds and hundreds of rounds from the

weapons of San Quentin guards and sharpshooters had been rapidly sprayed into and around the van. The judge's head had been blown off. The prosecutor had been critically wounded by San Quentin guard bullets. (Elaine Brown, *A Taste of Power*, NY: Anchor Books, 1992, p. 230)

8. Francis Cress Welsing interview in Kwaku Person-Lynn (ed.), *First Word*, NY: Harlem River Press, 1996, pp.74-75.

9. Holly Hill, SC: R & M Publishing Co., Inc, 1982 (2e), p.49.

10. The privileges accorded mulattoes throughout European history are lengthy but one can get a sense of their relative advantage in this society from the discussions in Winthrop D. Jordan, *The White Man's Burden*, NY: Oxford University Press, 1974, pp.83-86 and E. Franklin Frazier, *The Negro Family in the United States*, Chicago: University of Chicago Press, 1966 (first published 1939), pp.54, 55, 63, 64, 68, 145-146 and 147.

11. Chicago: Third World Press, 1987, pp.59 and 61. Especially look at pages 178-179 and 185-186 for a discussion of that historical collection of mulattoes who chose to side with their Afrikan mothers against the enemy of their people. This is but a very small sample of the documented evidence of a divisive conspiracy that finds itself wherever we find European invaders.

12. Nelson Mandela, *Long Walk to Freedom*, NY: Little, Brown and Company, 1994, Chancellor Williams, *The Destruction of Black Civilization: Great Issues of a Race From 4500 B.C. to 2000 A.D.*, Chicago: Third World Press, 1987, p.76. Also see Kathy Russell, Midge Wilson and Ronald Hall, *The Color Complex*, NY: Anchor Books, 1992, pp.60-61 for a short summary of the institutionalized racial classification system.

13. He wrote,

I have always threatened to write a massive book about...*The Role of the Bastard as a Factor in History.* How people have bastardized other people through their women and used the bastard to control them. Then having used the bastard, refuse to accept the bastard in the home of the father that created him and send him back to his mother's people to start confusion. (*Notes for An African World Revolution*, Trenton, NJ: Africa World Press, 1991, pp.252-253)

He also points to the direction he feels the analysis should go on pages 25, 46-47 and 100 in a collection of essays by Yosef ben-Jochannan and himself he edited entitled *New Dimensions in African History* (Trenton, NJ: Africa World Press, 1991).

14. *The Destruction of Black Civilization*, pp.50, 51, 71, 73-79, 154-155, 208, 218, 298 and 304.

15. *Defending the Spirit*, NY: Dutton, 1998, pp.75-77.

16. Although his discussion begins on page 33, he makes the same point about mulatto nationalism during the Haitian revolution.

They...did abolish slavery but forced the Blacks to remain on the plantations and work as before, but this time with wages. They also recruited many Blacks into their army but never let any rise above the rank of Captain and none were civilian office holders. The Mulattoes, however, were even more harsh on the Europeans, exterminating many and allowing them no positions of authority. (*The Irritated Genie*, Chicago: The Kemetic Institute, 1985, p.36)

17. While his statement must be assessed in the context of his *Destruction of Black Civilization* it has face value.

We should begin by drawing a vast African Circle of Honor around all those millions of Africans of mixed blood often referred to as Mulattoes, who from the earliest times to the present have stood steadfast and loyally identified with the race of their originally black mothers. They deserve special honor exactly because they did not have to do so when amalgamation of the races spread over Egypt and the Arabic world, and they had compelling reasons for *not* being identified with black-skinned Africans. For they were classified as "white" and, therefore, not subject to enslavement. (p.334)

18. Crawford, *"Racism, Colorism and Power,"* " *Frontline,* Vol. 3, No. 7, October 1999.

19. Francis Cress Welsing, *The Isis Papers*, Chicago: Third Word Press, 1991, p.xvii.

20. Chester Higgins, Jr., *Feeling the Spirit*, NY: Bantam Books, 1994, p.233.

21. Except for the truly insane, we must understand the politics of our oppressors for what it is.

Forgiveness is supposed to be a recognition or belief by the forgiver that the perpetrator's action will not occur again, that there will be a conscious attempt to never do whatever was done again. They have not stopped. Nor do they intend to. Second, forgetfulness downplays, to the oppressor's advantage, the roots of all revolutionary change – someone was wronged, with malice, forethought and beyond reason, and continues to be wronged in the same intolerable way....And, third, remembrance is a necessary and natural cleansing/healing ritual where the Maafa (the destruction of Afrikan civilization and culture and the enslavement, colonization and dehumanization of its people) is transformed into a wisdom that brings us as an Afrikan people back toward our rightful cultural Way. Our self-determined historical memory serves as a constant reminder to never let what happened to us happen again. (Larry D. Crawford, "The New Humanity," *The Faith Tribune*, March 12, 1999, p.5)

22. NY: Charles Scribner's Sons, 1992, pp.53-54.

23. Sterling Plumpp, *Black Rituals*, Chicago: Third World Press, 1972, p.94. John Henrik Clarke makes this same point when stating that, "We are veterans at making alliances with people who betray us, and the only reason that they betray us is that we do not control the apparatus of the alliances nor do we punish people who betray us" (*Notes*, p.39).

24. Plumpp, *Black Rituals*, p.96.

25. Malcolm X, *The Autobiography of Malcolm X*, NY: Ballantine Books, 1973, p.301.

26. *Race and Reparations*, Trenton, NJ: Africa World Press, 1996, pp.63-76, esp. pp.65-66.

27. The optimistic logic behind *Workforce 2000* (William B. Johnston and Arnold H. Packer, Indianapolis, IN: Hudson Institute, 1987) has already been stringently critiqued by Ronald B. Mincy. In summary, while the number of all jobs will shrink relative to the growth of the labor force age population, the number of jobs reserved for European males will remain constant, leaving the remaining, shrinking number as bones to be fought over by European females and every other kind of male and female that needs food and shelter and the respect only things can bring in the West ("Workforce 2000: Silver Bullet or Dud?: Job Structure Changes and Economic Prospects for Black Males in the 1990s," *Challenge*, No.1, Vol.2., May 1991, pp.50-76). Not as an aside, it should be noticed that even Mincy overlooked the competition being brought here by the European hordes flowing through the virtually unchecked Canadian border and transcontinental airports serving their fatherland.

28. Munford, *Race and Reparations*, 1996, p.259. Also see J.A. Rogers, *Nature Knows No Color-Line*, St. Petersburg. FL: Helga M. Rogers, 1952, pp.200-203 and Russell, Wilson and Hall, *The Color Complex*.

29. Munford, *Race and Reparations*, p.359.

Chapter 12

1. Stokely Carmichael and Charles V. Hamilton, *Black Power: The Politics of Liberation in America*, NY: Vintage Books, 1967, p.48.

2. James Baldwin